Break Your Trauma Cycle:
The 7 Archetypes of Transformation

A Groundbreaking Approach
to Accelerating Post Traumatic Growth

DR NAT GREEN

Copyright © 2024 Dr Nat Green

All rights reserved. No part of this publication may be reproduced, stored in or introduced into a retrieval system, or transmitted in any form or by any means, electronic, mechanical, photocopying, recording or otherwise, without the prior written permission from both the copyright owner and publisher. Any person who does any unauthorized act in relation to this publication may be liable to criminal prosecution and civil claims for damages. Enquiries should be made through the publisher.

Because of the dynamic nature of the internet, any web addresses or links contained in this book may be changed since original publication and may no longer be valid. The views expressed in this work are solely those of the author and do not necessarily reflect the views of the publisher, and the publisher hereby disclaims any responsibility for them.

Disclaimer

The author of this book does not dispense medical advice, nor prescribe the use of any technique as a form of treatment for physical, emotional, or medical problems without the advice of a physician, or your own psychologist either directly or indirectly. The intent of the author is only to offer information of a general nature to help you in your quest for improving your overall well-being.

All the information, techniques, skills, and concepts contained within this publication are of the nature of general comment only and are not in any way recommended as individual advice or treatment. The intent is to offer a variety of information to provide a wider range of choices now and in the future, recognising that we all have widely diverse circumstances and viewpoints. Should any reader choose to make use of the information contained herein, this is their decision and the author and publishers do not assume any responsibilities whatsoever under any condition or circumstances.

Published by Bettalife Solutions PL 2024
Publishing Partnership with Change Maker Press Pty Ltd

ISBN 978-1-7637600-0-4 (Paperback)
ISBN 978-1-7637600-1-1 (E-book)

Break Your Trauma Cycle:
The 7 Archetypes of Transformation

Dedication

To my amazing family – Warren, my loving husband whose endless support and encouragement uplift me daily; and my wonderful children, Alex and Maddie, who constantly inspire me, teach me, and push me to be the best version of myself. Thank you for standing by my side through it all, teaching me love, compassion, and, most of all, how to live life to the fullest every single day.

To my Mum, Sandra, who instilled in me commitment, dedication and above all, a fierce determination never to quit despite life's many twists and turns.

To my many mentors and teachers, who have nurtured, challenged and believed in me, showing me that it's more than okay to shine.

To my beautiful lifelong friend Karla, for your incredible encouragement and unparalleled editing skills throughout this heartfelt project. And to my Inner Circle of like-minded, impact-making girlfriends – thank you for believing in me, for lifting me up as a Collective through every challenge, and for keeping my vision alive. I thank you all from the bottom of my heart.

To you, the reader of this book, thank you for your courage to step forward despite the pain, to explore the deepest parts of yourself, and to embrace all that you are as you begin to truly Thrive.

Let this be your roadmap, guiding you to shine as brightly as you desire and to become the remarkable person you were always destined to be.

You've got this, here's to your success !

Dr. Nat

Contents

Dedication..iv

Introduction.. viii

CHAPTER 1
The Catalyst of Transformation
- Trauma and the Journey to Growth.. 1

CHAPTER 2
The Science of Trauma
- Rewiring the Brain, Body, and Soul.. 11

CHAPTER 3
The 7 Archetypes of Transformation©
- Your Guides from Trauma to Post-Traumatic Growth 25

CHAPTER 4
The Phoenix Riser
- Rising from the Ashes.. 41

CHAPTER 5
The Resilient Sage
- Wisdom from Wounds 57

CHAPTER 6
The Empowered Trailblazer
- Forging New Paths... 73

CHAPTER 7
The Reflective Orchestrator
– Healing Through Reflection 87

CHAPTER 8
The Authentic Warrior
- Strength in Vulnerability 101

CHAPTER 9
The Radiant Alchemist
- Transforming Pain into Purpose...115

CHAPTER 10
The Liberated Voyager
- Embracing Freedom...133

CHAPTER 11
Identifying Your Archetypes
- Keys to Post-Traumatic Growth...151

CHAPTER 12
Harnessing Archetypes
- Building Lasting Growth..171

CHAPTER 13
Combining Archetypes
- Holistic Healing 191

CHAPTER 14
Beyond Trauma
- The Future of Your Growth 205

CONCLUSION
Your Path to Thriving..215

About The Author..226

Introduction

For over three decades, I've been on the frontlines of trauma work- in the trenches alongside individuals whose lives have been shattered, guiding them through a maze of pain and devastation that follows profound trauma and adversity. Like many in the helping professions, I once believed that healing from trauma demanded years of unearthing memories and revisiting painful pasts. But as I witnessed countless individuals trapped in cycles of reliving their suffering rather than moving beyond it, a stark reality emerged and I couldn't ignore a fundamental truth: the current system is broken.

My conviction that there had to be a better way was cemented when I found myself on the other side of the couch, seeking help for my own profound trauma. Instead of healing, I encountered a system that left me feeling more isolated and betrayed than supported. The very professionals who had taken oaths to "do no harm" were instead reopening wounds and creating new ones. This personal journey through a broken system shattered me, but it also sparked a revolution in my approach to trauma healing work.

During a necessary sabbatical to heal, regroup, and re-examine everything I thought I knew about trauma and recovery, I found clarity. Through this period of detachment from the systems, I experimented with innovative accelerated coaching approaches, testing them first on myself. Through this process, I discovered patterns mirrored in the thousands of lives I'd encountered over my career. These patterns became the foundation for the Post-Traumatic Growth (PTG) Archetypes of Transformation©—a revolutionary framework that challenges the notion that trauma recovery must be a prolonged, painful process that proceeds at a glacial pace.

Here's what I've learned: Trauma doesn't just leave scars; it fundamentally shifts who we are at our core. The journey isn't about returning to who we once were—it's about becoming who we are truly meant to be. Many individuals complete traditional trauma treatment only to ask, "What now?" They may feel somewhat better but yearn for their former selves, unaware that this desire to return to the past and reclaim an old identity can become a trap. We can't go back. But we can grow forward.

This is where self-reconciliation becomes crucial - learning and accepting how trauma has altered us and finding peace with these changes. The Archetypes of Transformation© honour this process, giving permission to focus on "what's next" instead of remaining tethered to "what was" They provide a roadmap for those who feel lost or stuck, guiding them toward a new identity free from the weight of the past.

My mission is ambitious, and bold but clear: to end the unnecessary suffering associated with trauma in our world. While we can't prevent trauma and may never rid the world of trauma entirely, we can revolutionise and transform how people heal from it. The old methods that leave clients feeling stuck and therapists burnt out are no longer acceptable. We don't need endless years of treatment—we need a paradigm shift that recognises trauma not just as something to recover from, rather as an opportunity to evolve into our most powerful and authentic selves.

This book is your guide to that evolution, to living that life beyond trauma. Through these pages, discover your Archetype Profile©, embrace the hidden patterns, and take that courageous next step toward owning the remarkable person you're capable of becoming. Welcome to the revolution in trauma healing. Thank you for joining me on this journey.

Dr. Nat xx

Dr. Nat Green
Creator of the ABS Method®
and the Archetypes of Transformation©

CHAPTER 1

The Catalyst of Transformation

-

Trauma and the Journey to Growth

"Only when we are brave enough to explore the darkness will we discover the infinite power of our light."

— **Brené Brown**

When trauma enters our lives, it strikes deeply, leaving no stone unturned in its path. Its impact can ripple through every facet of our being, altering how we see ourselves, others, and our view of the world. For some of us, it feels like the foundation beneath our feet has crumbled. The world we once knew no longer exists or has changed forever. In these moments, we become raw, vulnerable, and open to the harshest realities. Trauma can break us down, strip us of the security we once took for granted and challenge our sense of identity and who we are at our very core.

But what if I told you that trauma, as devastating as it can be, holds within it the seeds of transformation? What if trauma could be the very catalyst that pushes us into a new realm of existence and possibilities—one where we don't just survive, but we actually thrive?

This journey from Trauma to Post Traumatic Growth (PTG) is not an easy one. It requires us to delve deep within ourselves, to confront the shadows, and to unearth our strength. However, with the right tools, it's a journey that can lead to profound healing, personal growth, and even a renewed sense of purpose and identity.

In my decades of working with trauma survivors, I've seen firsthand the pain and struggle that trauma brings. Yet, I've also witnessed something extraordinary: the power of the human spirit to rise from the ashes and the resilience of those who have faced unimaginable pain and have come out the other side, not just mended, but transformed.

This transformation, often referred to as Post Traumatic Growth, is a testament to the personal attributes and strength that lie within each of us. We are all able to access it when given the right guidance, support, tools and strategies.

My own personal trauma journey led me to experience the depths of despair and saw me navigating a challenging and often lonely path.

Reflecting on my own experience and those of the thousands of individuals I've had the privilege to work with, I began to recognise patterns in how people respond to trauma and what facilitates or stunts their subsequent growth.

Identifying these patterns has led to the creation of my **Trauma Archetypes of Transformation©**. From a psychology perspective, these are innate patterns of thought and behaviour that strive for realisation within one's environment and provide distinct paths of growth that represent the unique ways in which people can heal, rebuild and thrive after trauma.

Defining Trauma and Its Deep Impact

Before we can truly appreciate the transformative power of trauma, we must understand its nature.

Trauma isn't just a singular event; it's an experience that overwhelms our ability to cope, leaving us feeling disconnected, disoriented, powerless and losing control. Trauma can stem from a variety of sources—whether it's a single life-altering incident, repeated experiences of abuse or neglect, or even more subtle, ongoing circumstances that erode our sense of safety over time.

It might be complex trauma from chronic and prolonged overwhelming events or experiences, such as through domestic violence, or emergency service workers exposed to multiple traumas, or developmental trauma from early onset as an infant, child or adolescent. It may be through vicarious trauma where we've heard others' trauma stories such as with helping professionals.

The impact of trauma is multifaceted. It can shatter our sense of self, fragment our thoughts, and invade our emotions. Trauma isn't just something we "get over" or "move past." It imprints itself on our psyche, our nervous system, and becomes ingrained in our very being. Often, trauma is accompanied by negative emotions including deep feelings of guilt, shame, hurt, and self-blame. It clouds our judgment, has us questioning ourselves and our capacity, distorts our worldview, and holds us captive in its grip.

For years I felt this suffocating weight, and this was further compounded by systems that left me completely powerless. My own trauma brought me to my knees, leaving me questioning my identity and my purpose. But over time, I began to see glimmers of light—moments of clarity that have helped me realise that trauma didn't have to define me. Instead, it could shape me and become a catalyst for my growth.

Instead of my trauma dictating who I was, I used it to discover who I could become and am now paying that forward for others.

Post Traumatic Growth: The Promise Beyond Pain

When we talk about trauma, we often focus on the damage it causes, but far less frequently do we acknowledge the growth that can follow.

Post Traumatic Growth is the process by which individuals who have experienced trauma begin to see new possibilities for their lives. It's the shift from being broken by trauma to being empowered by it and having hope. This transformation doesn't erase the pain of what happened—it integrates it. The scars remain, but they become part of a larger story of resilience and strength.

Post Traumatic Growth is a psychological concept that refers to the positive psychological changes and personal development that can occur as a result of struggling with - and overcoming - trauma or significant adversity.

It involves a transformation that leads someone to a higher level of functioning and a deeper sense of meaning and purpose in life. Usually we see increased personal strength, improved relationships, new possibilities and a greater appreciation for life as well as spiritual and existential growth.

Post Traumatic Growth is about reclaiming our lives after trauma and recognising that, despite the hardships, we are not just a survivor—we are a thriver. This shift is both profound and personal, and no two journeys look the same. For some, Post Traumatic Growth might mean deepening relationships, while for others, it's about rediscovering a sense of purpose, embracing their spirituality, or stepping into a new identity.

And that's where my Trauma Archetypes of Transformation© come into play. Each archetype represents a unique path to growth—a way of navigating the complexities of trauma, tapping into and drawing on your inner strength.

These archetypes are not about fitting into a box; they are about helping you understand your journey in a way that resonates deeply with who you are at your core.

Introducing the Trauma Archetypes of Transformation©

The Trauma Archetypes of Transformation© are more than just labels—they are mirrors reflecting the diverse ways in which we adapt, grow, and evolve after trauma. Each archetype embodies certain strengths, challenges, and potential growth paths.

Understanding your archetype isn't about limiting yourself; it's about gaining insight into the ways in which you can best heal and thrive and how to minimise your specific challenges so your strengths can be activated and serve you as well as possible.

It's about knowing your strengths, acknowledging your unique challenges, and finding the tools that will propel you forward.

As we move through the chapters ahead, I will introduce you to each of these seven Trauma Archetypes:

- **The Phoenix Riser©**: Rising from the ashes, this archetype symbolises rebirth, renewal, and the ability to transform pain into power.
- **The Resilient Sage©**: Guided by wisdom and inner peace, the Sage is about cultivating resilience through insight and reflection.
- **The Empowered Trailblazer©**: Bold and fearless, the Trailblazer paves the way for others, using their experiences to inspire and lead.
- **The Reflective Orchestrator©**: Introspective and thoughtful, the Orchestrator carefully plans their healing journey, aligning their inner world with their outer experiences.
- **The Authentic Warrior©**: Fierce and true to themselves, the Warrior embraces vulnerability as strength and stands tall in the face of adversity.
- **The Radiant Alchemist©**: Transmuting pain into purpose, the Alchemist finds meaning in suffering and turns it into gold.

- **The Liberated Voyager©**: Embracing freedom and discovery, the Voyager embarks on a journey of self-exploration and transformation.

Each archetype offers a pathway forward, with its own unique gifts and challenges. As you explore these archetypes, you'll begin to see yourself within them. You'll recognise your strengths, confront your fears, and, ultimately, embrace your power. It is highly likely that one Archetype will be your dominant one and you will probably resonate with others too.

Your top 3 archetypes become your Archetype Profile©.

A Journey of Empowerment

This book is not just about learning—it's about becoming. My goal is to empower you to deeply understand and identify who you are now as a result of your experiences and connect with this version of you. Then, step into who you are and embrace your archetype fully. When you understand your story, rediscover your purpose and step fully into your Post Traumatic Growth, then and only then are you free to write your next chapter.

Whether you identify as a Phoenix Riser, a Resilient Sage, or any of the other archetypes, this journey is yours to shape.

Trauma may have touched your life, but it does not need to limit and define your future. In fact, you have the power to transform it into something beautiful, meaningful, and even life-affirming. Together, we will explore how to harness the wisdom of each archetype, break free from old patterns, and cultivate a life of resilience, joy, and purpose.

As we embark on this journey, remember, you are not alone. You are supported by countless others who, just like you, are rising from the ashes, standing tall, and reclaiming and shining their light in this world.

It's time to embrace your archetype, honour your growth, and move boldly into the future you so rightly deserve.

Let's begin.

CHAPTER 2

The Science of Trauma
-
Rewiring the Brain, Body, and Soul

> "The body keeps the score. If the body knows the truth, the mind cannot flee from it."
>
> **- Bessel van der Kolk**

Trauma doesn't just live in the mind. It's not simply an emotional wound that we can tuck away neatly into a drawer of the past and close. It's pervasive, all-consuming, and it ultimately changes us on a fundamental level.

Trauma alters the brain, imprints itself within our body, and seeps into our very soul. It is critical to understand that trauma, when left unresolved, can embed itself in every facet of our being.

Yet, here's the powerful truth: just as trauma rewires us, we have the ability to rewire ourselves in return.

Through my own journey with trauma, combined with my years of professional work, I've seen this over and over. Yes, trauma changes us, but it doesn't have to be the end of our story.

We have the incredible potential to reshape our brains through changing our neural pathways, heal our bodies through releasing our stored trauma, and restore our spirit and sense of self. However, to do so, we must first understand what trauma does to us on a physiological and psychological level, and from there we can harness the tools that will allow us to heal, grow, and ultimately to thrive.

Trauma and the Brain: Rewiring Survival

When we talk about trauma, we must begin with the brain. Trauma leaves an indelible mark on the brain, fundamentally altering its structure and function and literally rewiring it.

At the heart of it all lies our fight, flight, and freeze responses—primal mechanisms designed to protect us from danger. When trauma strikes, our brain automatically kicks into survival mode.

The **amygdala**, the part of the brain responsible for detecting threats, becomes hyperactive in the face of trauma, constantly scanning for danger even when none is present. It sounds the alarm over and over, forcing us to relive the trauma in different ways, and this heightened state of vigilance can activate flashbacks, anxiety, and hypervigilance, essentially trapping us in a cycle of survival mode.

Meanwhile, the **prefrontal cortex**, which is the rational, "thinking" part of our brain responsible for decision-making, starts to shut down leaving us feeling overwhelmed, unable to process emotions effectively, and struggling with irrational fears or intrusive thoughts.

It's as though trauma hijacks our brain, making it harder to think clearly, regulate our emotions, and respond to life in a balanced way, through choosing reactions over considered responses. You may notice this in yourself when you feel constantly on edge, easily startled, or as though you're reliving the traumatic event repeatedly in your mind.

You're not "overreacting" or "too sensitive"—rather, your brain is trying to protect you the best way it knows how. Yet, here's the problem: when the brain stays in this heightened state for too long, it begins to work against us.

However, we can retrain our brains to move beyond survival and to respond differently. The concept of **neuroplasticity** shows us that our brains are adaptable.

Through practices such as mindfulness, neuroplasticity exercises (like doing puzzles, creating art, learning an instrument) and nervous system regulation techniques (like Trauma and Tension Release Exercises TRE) we can gradually calm the amygdala and reactivate and strengthen our prefrontal cortex.

These practices teach our brain that it is safe again, allowing us to move from living in a constant state of survival to a place of safety and potential growth where we can actually thrive.

But the brain is not alone in this journey; trauma also resides in the body.

Trauma in the Body: Holding the Pain Within

You may have heard the phrase, "The body keeps the score."

Trauma doesn't just reside in our minds; it lodges itself in our body's tissues, creating patterns of tension, pain and other chronic symptoms that continue long after the traumatic event has ended. Our bodies continue to carry the weight of it.

The work of Bessel van der Kolk (2014) highlights how overwhelming experiences affect the development of brain, mind and body awareness. Chronic pain, fatigue, tension, digestive issues and autoimmune diseases—these are all ways the body cries out for help, signalling that the trauma has yet to be processed.

For years, I carried my trauma at a deep cellular level within my own body. There were moments where I'd feel exhausted, unable to pinpoint why, or where I'd feel a tightening and random pain in various parts of my body, as if it was constantly bracing for impact. In those moments, I wasn't always aware that trauma had left its imprint on me physically as much as emotionally.

Our bodies are brilliant communicators—they will send us signals, whether through tension, discomfort, or even illness, when something deep inside has yet to be addressed. We need to learn to listen more effectively to these messages.

There has been significant development within the field of neuroscience, particularly in the last 10-15 years. One that I especially have resonated with is the concept of the three brains, in particular the work of Marvin Oka and Grant Soosalu (2012). We have complex, adaptive and fully functional neural networks or 'brains' in our head, our heart and our gut.

The body often holds onto trauma in these three critical areas — the head, the heart, and the gut — which can be thought of as our "three brains." Each of these areas plays a unique role in processing trauma and healing from it.

1. **The Head (Cognitive Brain):** This is the master of processes, the seat of our conscious thought, logic, perception, analysis and reasoning. When trauma disrupts this part of our brain, we struggle with decision-making, memory recall, and regulation of our emotions. Neuroplasticity exercises, or mindfulness practices, can help to restore the function of this brain.

2. **The Heart (Emotional Brain):** The heart is more than just a pump; it plays a significant role in our emotional health. The heart has its own "mini-brain," with its nervous system containing over 40,000 neurons capable of processing and responding to emotions. This is where we process deep emotions, what we feel and the connections we have with others. It is also where our values, dreams, desires and aspirations lie. Trauma can disrupt the harmony of this brain, leading to feelings of disconnection, anxiety, and emotional overwhelm. Techniques like heart-focused breathing, meditation, and fostering self-compassion can help to heal and regulate the emotional brain.

3. **The Gut (Instinctive Brain):** The gut contains approximately 500 million neurons, often referred to as the "enteric nervous system" or the "second brain". This extensive network of neurons plays a crucial role in regulating digestive functions, communicating with the brain, and influencing our mood and overall well-being (Furness, J. B. 2012). It plays a significant role in our instinctual responses and emotional health. Our gut is where our intuition and our core identity lie, as

well as our sense of self. It is also responsible for safety and protection, boundaries and impulse actions, as well as upholding our immune system. Trauma can disrupt gut function, leading to symptoms like digestive issues, nausea, or "gut feelings" of fear, anxiety or unease. Healing the gut brain involves practices like mindful eating, yoga, and body-oriented therapies to restore balance.

When we experience trauma, at least one of the three brains becomes disconnected. Disconnection between the three brains creates imbalance, dysfunction and conflict and restricts growth and contribution (Green, 2017).

The good news is that just as the body holds trauma, it also holds the key to releasing it. By working with these three brains — the head, the heart, and the gut — we can address trauma from a comprehensive, whole-person perspective.

Techniques like TRE (Tension & Trauma Releasing Exercises), yoga, somatic experiencing, and breathwork can help to release trapped energy and tension. By working *with* our body, rather than *against* it, we begin to unearth the trauma that's been stored there and release it in a way that brings deep healing and relief, as we help the body to find its voice, to "speak" and finally let go.

The Soul's Wound: Trauma and Spiritual Disconnection

Trauma doesn't stop at the mind and body, and while trauma rewires the brain and the body, it also penetrates the soul, severing our connection to a sense of purpose or something greater.

When trauma strikes, it can leave us feeling adrift, isolated, and questioning the very meaning of life. We start to doubt ourselves, the world around us, and the very essence of life itself.

This spiritual disconnection can be one of the most painful aspects of trauma. It often leaves us with a sense of existential loneliness and despair, doubting so much, including our place in the world.

However, it's important to emphasise here that disconnection doesn't mean that we've lost ourselves entirely. It means that we've simply lost our way. And the beauty of the soul is that it always knows how to find its way back home.

It is in this darkness that the potential for deep, spiritual growth and healing emerges. Trauma, whilst extremely painful, can also serve as a catalyst for reconnecting with our soul's true purpose.

In my own healing, connecting to and clearing out old wounds and reconnecting with my soul became one of the most profound aspects of my journey. I discovered and learned to rebuild my sense of purpose, to find meaning in the pain, and to allow the learnings and lessons from my trauma experience to guide me on the path I'm now travelling.

Through the lens of self-compassion with practices like meditation, journalling, and deep self-reflection, we can begin to rebuild our sense of purpose, find meaning in our pain, and view trauma as a guide - rather than a burden.

When we tend to the wounds of our soul, we rekindle our connection to our higher selves and something greater than us - whatever that may be - and we begin to see the light again, even in the darkest of times. This is possible for each and every one of us.

Letting Go: The Journey Through the Three Brains

From my work in the *Key to Freedom* book (Green, 2017), and its application in my own life and those of my clients, I've come to understand that letting go is not a passive process: it's an active, conscious decision that involves all three brains.

A lot of the deeper work is done at an unconscious level, though with conscious awareness of the changes. Trauma often makes us hold on to pain, fear, memories, and our survival instincts because holding on feels safer than facing the unknown.

But to truly heal, we must learn to let go.

1. The Head Brain's Role in Letting Go

Letting go requires the cognitive brain to make sense of and reframe past experiences, challenge old beliefs, and embrace new narratives. Techniques like reframing conscious thoughts, practicing gratitude, and engaging in reflective journalling help in letting go of limiting thoughts and beliefs that trauma has etched into our consciousness. However, the true power is engaging in the deeper work at an unconscious level and this led me to develop my Accelerated Breakthrough Strategies (ABS) Method ®.

2. **The Heart Brain's Role in Letting Go**

At the heart level, letting go involves emotional processing and release. This means allowing ourselves to feel fully — to grieve, to be angry, to feel joy — without judgment. By practicing self-compassion, empathy, and emotional awareness, we allow the heart brain to release the emotions that have been trapped by trauma, opening space for new, healing emotions to emerge. This also allows us to connect to our deep values and get clear on what really matters to us and what values we want to guide us through life.

3. **The Gut Brain's Role in Letting Go**

The gut brain, often the keeper of our instincts and intuition, needs reassurance that letting go of trauma is safe. Through mindful practices like breathwork, gentle movement, and grounding exercises, we can help calm the instinctive fears that hold us back. Trusting our gut, re-establishing our body's sense of safety, and nurturing a healthy gut-brain connection are all essential steps in the process of letting go. This is where we get absolute clarity around our sense of self and our core identity.

The Potential for Healing and Growth: Moving Beyond Survival

Here's where things can really start to shift. While trauma rewires the brain, body, and soul, healing is both possible and inevitable when we 'follow the breadcrumbs' and commit to proven practices.

Our brains are wonderfully adaptive through the neuroplasticity process, where we can rewire our thinking, heal our emotional wounds and break free from the survival responses that trauma left behind.

Our bodies, when given the chance to process, can release our stored trauma and feel lighter and healthier. And our souls once reconnected can help us find purpose in the pain and guide us toward a life filled with meaning, growth and possibilities...and ultimately to our purpose.

Healing is a journey that involves all three of our "brains" working in harmony — the head, the heart, and the gut becoming integrated and learning to truly communicate with each other.

This journey is deeply personal and unique, yet it follows universal principles of growth and resilience. It is here that the **Trauma Archetypes** © come into play.

Each archetype offers specific insights into how trauma affects us individually and provides a unique pathway and roadmap for healing, reflecting the different ways trauma affects us and how we can reclaim our power, find our voice, and grow beyond our wounds.

Whether you see yourself as a Phoenix Riser, an Empowered Trailblazer, or any of the other archetypes, your healing journey will be unique, and the key lies in understanding how to let go of trauma's grip and move forward to a place of empowerment so you have the ability to rewrite the narrative of your trauma.

Conclusion: Reclaiming Your Power

Trauma is powerful, but so are you.

Yes, it may have changed the way your brain functions, the way your body feels, and even the way your soul connects—yet it does not have to define you. You have the capacity to heal, to grow, and to emerge stronger than ever before.

By understanding the science of trauma, embracing the wisdom of our three brains and exploring our unique Trauma Archetypes of Transformation© we begin to reclaim our power and write a new story of healing, growth and thriving.

We see trauma for what it is—not as something that defines us, but as something that can guide us toward profound personal growth. As we continue to explore the Trauma Archetypes©, know that this journey is about understanding that while trauma may have rewired us, we have the tools, the strength, and the wisdom to rewire ourselves into a version that is stronger, wiser, and more resilient than ever before.

You are not broken. Letting go is the bridge between surviving and thriving. You are evolving. And with every step you take on this journey, you move closer to becoming the incredible, empowered, thriving person you are meant to be.

CHAPTER 3

The 7 Archetypes of Transformation©

-

Your Guides from Trauma to Post-Traumatic Growth

"Although the world is full of suffering, it is also full of the overcoming of it."

—Helen Keller

The fact you're here reading this book means there's a chance you've experienced trauma, or you're supporting someone who has. You know it has the power to reshape every single part of your life.

However, here's the truth I want you to understand and embrace: trauma may *shape* you, but it doesn't *define* you.

As we've already acknowledged, trauma may have shaken you to your core, and it also holds the potential to mould you into a version of yourself that's stronger, wiser, and more resilient than you ever could have imagined. And as we embark on this journey of healing and growth, you don't have to go it alone.

We've talked about trauma and the impact that trauma has on our mind, our body and our soul and we've also talked about Post Traumatic Growth (PTG), which is the notion that people can not only heal from trauma but actually experience positive life changes as a result of their struggles.

And here's the really fascinating part: PTSD and Post Traumatic Growth can co-exist (Dell'Osso L, et al 2022). You can still struggle with trauma symptoms while simultaneously experiencing growth. It's not an either/or situation, rather a both/and journey.

The key lies in finding meaning in your experiences and using that meaning as a catalyst for growth to eventually move beyond your trauma to a place of thriving.

This is where our exciting new concept comes in – the Trauma Archetypes of Transformation© to Post Traumatic Growth.

These 7 archetypes are more than just labels—they are powerful symbols of different aspects of growth and healing. They are reflections of who you are and how you respond to the pain, struggle, and transformation that trauma brings into your life. They serve as guides, illuminating various paths forward and helping you tap into strengths you might not even know you possess.

Each archetype represents your unique pathway through trauma and into post-traumatic growth, and each one holds the keys to unlocking your greatest potential.

As we explore these archetypes in depth, you'll find yourself reflected in them. You'll recognise yourself in their narratives, draw upon their strengths, and use them as a compass for your own growth journey. These archetypes aren't just theoretical concepts – they'll provide practical tools that can accelerate your healing and help you step into your full potential.

Perhaps you see yourself as a Phoenix Riser, boldly rising from the ashes of your pain. Or maybe you resonate more with the deep wisdom of the Resilient Sage, whose experiences have forged a profound understanding of life.

Whatever your archetype, it's important to know that there is no wrong way to heal—only your way. These archetypes are here to guide you, to empower you, and to help you recognise the incredible strengths you already possess.

You are currently travelling on a hero's journey. The trauma you've experienced doesn't define you – it's simply part of your story. What defines you is the courage you show every day in facing your challenges, the resilience you demonstrate in moving forward, and the wisdom you gain along the way.

Are you ready to meet your Inner Heroes?

First, let me share a little secret with you. These archetypes? They're not just theoretical constructs or characters from ancient myths. They're alive within you right now. They are the fundamental units of the human mind. They are the living system of reactions and attributes that determine an individual's life in invisible ways. They also represent the incredible potential for growth and healing that you already possess, even if you can't quite see it yet.

Each one offers a distinct pathway to healing, and as you learn about them, I encourage you to reflect on your own journey. You may identify with one or more archetypes, and that's completely okay.

You will likely have a dominant Archetype that you resonate most closely with, and another two that you can see considerable parts of yourself in. Your top 3 Archetypes will become your Trauma Archetype Profile©.

It's important to remember that healing is never a straight line, and you'll likely find that different aspects of your personality and experience align with different archetypes at different times.

As someone who has walked the path from trauma to post traumatic growth, and didn't have a roadmap to guide me, I can tell you that recognising, developing and embracing these archetypes has been a game-changer in my own journey. And I believe they can be for you, too.

Let's dive in and introduce you to these powerful seven archetypes.

1. The Phoenix Riser

The Phoenix Riser embodies the power of transformation. Much like the mythical phoenix, you too rise from the ashes of your trauma, stronger and more powerful than before.

When life knocks you down, you don't stay there for long. You're driven by an unshakable belief in your ability to overcome adversity and emerge victorious.

But here's the thing about the Phoenix Riser: while your resilience and inner strength is undeniable, there's often a layer of exhaustion hidden just beneath the surface. Rising from the ashes certainly is not easy, and it's so important to give yourself permission to rest and heal.

Your strength comes from knowing that even in the darkest moments, there's always a spark of hope within you that can't be snuffed out. And with that hope, you rise— time and time again.

As a Phoenix Riser, you also inspire others through your courage and your determination. You are living proof that no matter how deep the pain, you can always emerge from your trauma stronger, more vibrant and rebuild and begin anew.

2. The Resilient Sage

The Resilient Sage is the embodiment of wisdom, born through your experiences. You've been through the fire, and it has given you a deep understanding of life's complexities.

Trauma may have scarred you, but it has also made you wise beyond your years. You have a gift for seeing the bigger picture and finding meaning in even the most difficult of circumstances.

Your strength lies in your ability to stay grounded and calm, even in the midst of chaos. However, be mindful, your wisdom is undoubtedly a double-edged sword. Sometimes, you may retreat into your thoughts, using your intellect as a shield to avoid the raw emotions of your trauma. Healing for you comes not only through understanding but through allowing yourself to feel deeply and authentically.

As a Resilient Sage, you have the capacity to not only endure but to gain profound insights and to use your insights to guide yourself and others on their own healing journeys. You are a beacon of calm and clarity, showing that with perspective and patience, growth is always possible.

3. The Empowered Trailblazer

The Empowered Trailblazer is a force of nature. You don't just survive trauma—you forge new paths in its wake.

Your strength lies in your ability to take charge, break free from old patterns, and create a life that is uniquely yours. You are braver than you know and refuse to be held back by your past - instead, you use it as fuel to propel yourself forward.

Your determination can sometimes come at a cost. In your drive to keep pushing ahead, you may forget to pause and process the pain that's still lingering beneath the surface.

Remember that healing isn't a race—it's a journey. You will benefit the most from giving yourself the grace to move at your own pace and know that it's okay to slow down and reflect when you need to.

As an Empowered Trailblazer, you inspire others by stepping beyond the boundaries of your comfort zone and showing them that they, too, can carve out their own path to healing. Your courage to venture into the unknown reminds us that our pasts do not define our future.

4. The Reflective Orchestrator

The Reflective Orchestrator is all about balance and harmony. Life after trauma can feel chaotic, but you have the power to create harmony from the discord.

You have an incredible ability to navigate trauma with grace, carefully weaving together the many aspects of your life to create something beautiful and meaningful. You are introspective and thoughtful, always seeking to understand the deeper lessons that trauma has to offer.

However, your desire for harmony can sometimes lead you to avoid confrontation or uncomfortable emotions. You may often find yourself focusing on others' needs while neglecting your own.

Your healing journey involves finding the courage to prioritise yourself and face the difficult emotions head-on.

As a Reflective Orchestrator, your ability to create balance and beauty in the midst of chaos is a gift. This archetype represents your ability to reflect, integrate, and orchestrate a new symphony for your life. You remind us that even in the aftermath of trauma, we have the power to shape our lives with intention and purpose.

5. The Authentic Warrior

The Authentic Warrior is fierce, bold, and unafraid to face the truth. You have a deep commitment to living authentically, no matter the cost.

Trauma often makes us hide parts of ourselves, but this archetype embodies the strength to be unapologetically yourself. Trauma may have tested your strength, but it has also revealed your unshakable sense of integrity.

You fight for what you believe in, and you refuse to be anything other than your true self.

However, your strength can sometimes become a shield, protecting you from the vulnerability that's necessary for deep healing. Remember that true strength comes not just from fighting your battles, but from allowing yourself to be open and honest about your pain.

Healing for you involves embracing both your strength and your softness.

As an Authentic Warrior, you are a powerful example of what it means to live with courage and conviction. You show others that even in the face of trauma, we can stand tall and be true to ourselves. For you it's about facing life with honesty, integrity, and fierce self-acceptance.

6. The Radiant Alchemist

The Radiant Alchemist has a unique gift for turning pain into purpose. You don't just heal—you transform. Trauma becomes your catalyst for change, and you have an incredible ability to find light even in the darkest of times.

You're a natural healer, both for yourself and for others, and you radiate a sense of hope and possibility wherever you go.

However, your gift for transformation can sometimes lead you to take on too much. In your desire to help others, you may forget to tend to your own needs and have trouble setting and holding boundaries.

Your healing journey involves learning to balance your desire to heal the world with the need to care for yourself.

As a Radiant Alchemist, your natural ability to create beauty and meaning out of pain is nothing short of magical. You inspire others to believe in the power of transformation and remind us that even in the darkest moments, there is always light to be found.

This archetype symbolises the process of taking the lead with your trauma and turning it into valuable new meaning and direction.

7. The Liberated Voyager

The Liberated Voyager is all about freedom and exploration. Trauma may have confined you, but you refuse to be held captive by it.

You have a deep desire to break free from the limitations of your past and to explore new horizons, both within yourself and in the world around you. You are a seeker, always looking for new ways to grow and evolve.

However, your quest for freedom can sometimes leave you feeling untethered. In your desire to move forward, you may struggle with feeling grounded and connected to the present moment.

Your healing journey involves finding the balance between exploration and stillness, allowing yourself to be fully present in your life as it unfolds, rather than impatiently wanting to jump too far ahead.

As a Liberated Voyager, your adventurous spirit and thirst for growth remind us that healing is a journey, and not a destination. It's about breaking free from the chains of your past, disentangling from what might be keeping you stuck, and embarking on a voyage of self-discovery and growth.

You inspire others to embrace the unknown and to trust in the process of transformation.

Conclusion: Discovering Your Archetype

Now that you've met the 7 Trauma Archetypes, take a moment to reflect on which one you feel resonates with you the most.

Remember, there's no right or wrong answer. You may see yourself in multiple archetypes, or you may find that different aspects of your personality align with different archetypes at different times. That's the beauty of this journey—your healing is uniquely yours, and these archetypes are simply here to guide you along the way.

Now, you might be wondering, "Do I have to embody all of these archetypes?" The beautiful answer is no. These archetypes represent different aspects of growth and healing, and you might find that you resonate more strongly with some than others.

That's perfectly okay! The key is to recognise that all of these potentials exist within you, waiting to be awakened and developed.

Think of these archetypes as different facets of a diamond. Each one reflects light in its own unique way, but together, they create something breathtakingly beautiful and resilient.

In the same way, each archetype represents a different aspect of post-traumatic growth:

🦋 The Phoenix Riser speaks to our ability to rebuild and transform.

🦋 The Resilient Sage embodies the wisdom we gain through our experiences.

🦋 The Empowered Trailblazer represents our capacity to move forward and inspire others.

🦋 The Reflective Orchestrator symbolizes our power to create meaning and balance.

🦋 The Authentic Warrior stands for our journey towards self-acceptance and integrity.

🦋 The Radiant Alchemist embodies our ability to find purpose in our pain.

🦋 And the Liberated Voyager represents our quest for freedom and self-discovery.

These archetypes don't exist in isolation. They're deeply interconnected, often working in tandem to support your growth. For example, the wisdom of your inner Resilient Sage might fuel the courage of your Empowered Trailblazer. The transformative power of your Phoenix Riser might ignite the creativity of your Radiant Alchemist.

As you journey through this book, you'll have the opportunity to explore each archetype in depth. You'll discover how they manifest and show up in your life, how to tap into their unique strengths, and how to use them as guides on your path to post-traumatic growth.

Remember that embracing these archetypes isn't about becoming someone new. It's about recognising and nurturing the incredible strengths and aptitudes that already exist within you.

It's about seeing yourself through new eyes and realising that your trauma doesn't define you – your growth does.

No matter which archetypes you identify with, know that you have the inner strength, wisdom, and resilience to move from trauma to post-traumatic growth. These archetypes are your allies on this journey, helping you to unlock your potential and step into the fullness of who you are. Understanding these archetypes and delving more deeply into discovering them can undoubtedly be key to accelerating your transition through to Post Traumatic Growth.

In the chapters that follow, we'll dive deep into each archetype. We'll explore their characteristics, examine real-life examples, and share practical exercises to help you connect with and embody each one.

So, take a deep breath. Feel the potential stirring within you. Your inner Phoenix is ready to rise, your inner Sage is whispering wisdom, your inner Trailblazer is itching to move forward.

Can you feel it? That's the power of your Post Traumatic Growth Archetypes, ready to guide you towards healing, growth, and a life more beautiful and meaningful than you ever imagined possible.

CHAPTER 4

The Phoenix Riser

—

Rising from the Ashes

"Like a phoenix, she will rise from the ashes of despair and soar."

— Lorna Jackie Wilson

When you think of the phoenix rising, you likely imagine a brilliant bird soaring upward from a fiery blaze— its singed wings spread wide and strong, propelling it forward and rising away from the possible harm that awaits and from the flames that once threatened to consume it. In mythology, the phoenix rises reborn from its own ashes, transformed rather than destroyed by the fire.

The Phoenix Riser archetype embodies this same power of transformation through adversity. It symbolises the incredible strength and resilience that trauma survivors possess when they rise from the ashes of their experiences and begin to rebuild their lives one step at a time. To rise as a Phoenix Riser is to embrace the pain, acknowledge the struggle, and still choose to soar.

This archetype holds a special place in my heart, because I've seen it in so many survivors I've worked with, and in my own journey too. As a Phoenix Riser, they've undoubtedly been through deep, soul-crushing trauma and faced life's darkest moments, and they've dug deep, found the courage and chosen to rise.

The Journey of the Phoenix Riser

Phoenix Risers have chosen not to let their trauma break them, but rather to use it as fuel for their transformation. The fiery ashes of the past don't *define* them; they *refine* them. And with every rise, they have become stronger, more empowered, and more capable of creating the life they truly want.

They have proven to themselves time and again that they are strong and capable and able to endure anything, even the most trying of times.

This rise is not a one-time event. It's a continuous journey—a cycle of falling, rising, transforming, and evolving. As a Phoenix Riser, they carry the weight of the past and hold the power to reshape it into something that fuels their future. They take life's deepest pains and turn them into wisdom and strength. This is the essence of post-traumatic growth: not just surviving trauma but thriving in its wake.

The Core Strengths of the Phoenix Riser

A Phoenix Riser's greatest strength is their **resilience**. Life may have thrown them into the fire, however, they have the unique ability to pull themselves up and keep going, no matter how many times they've been knocked down. They are the embodiment of strength and determination, and their ability to persevere in the face of adversity sets them apart.

But resilience is not their only strength - there's so much more to the Phoenix Riser. They are also **highly adaptable**. Trauma forces us to change, and whether we like it or not, we are never the same person after a significant trauma. The Phoenix Riser has mastered the art of adapting to these changes. They've learned to navigate their new realities, adjust to different circumstances, and still move forward despite all that has been thrown their way. This adaptability is what allows them to keep rising, no matter how often life may try to drag them back down.

One of the most powerful aspects of the Phoenix Riser is their ability to become a **beacon of hope** for others, shining their light for all to see. Through their journey they serve as a powerful example of what is possible when we refuse to let trauma define us. They are constantly seeking ways to grow, transform and to heal.

Their story of transformation offers a light for others still in the depths of their struggles, showing them that it is possible to heal, grow, and thrive. They are a living testament to the power of post-traumatic growth and inspire those around them to believe in their own capacity for healing, even when it feels like all hope has been lost. Their story is one of triumph, and through their transformation, they light the way for others to follow.

The Emotional Landscape of the Phoenix Riser

The emotional journey of the Phoenix Riser is complex and multi-layered. On one hand, there's the immense pride and gratitude that comes with having risen from their lowest points. They've faced the fire and still emerged stronger, and that is something to celebrate.

However, being a Phoenix Riser also means navigating feelings of deep **weariness**. The constant cycle of rising from the ashes can be exhausting, and many Phoenix Risers carry a profound sense of fatigue. They've been through so much, and while they're proud of their ability to overcome, there's often a lingering sense of exhaustion from the constant need to rebuild. They may feel like they're always in "survival mode," never quite able to fully relax or let their guard down. Burnout can creep in as they continually push themselves without pause.

This weariness is compounded by the Phoenix Riser's tendency to rely heavily on their **strength** as a shield. They've become so adept at rising from the ashes that they may struggle with vulnerability. For some Phoenix Risers, showing weakness or asking for help can feel impossible. They've been burned before and trusting others can feel too risky when they've spent so much time and energy building themselves back up. This fear of vulnerability can become an emotional anchor, dragging them down and preventing them from experiencing true healing.

The Challenges of the Phoenix Riser

While their strength and resilience are undeniable, a Phoenix Riser comes with their own set of challenges. Chief among them is the tendency to push forward without pausing for **rest**. They've generally become so accustomed to rising again and again that they may struggle to slow down, even when the body and mind are crying out for a break. There's often a fear that if they stop, the flames of their trauma will consume them once more, so they keep rising and moving forward—often at the expense of their own well-being.

We often see chronic health conditions developing in a Phoenix Riser as a result of this relentless drive. We know the body carries trauma, and without rest and regulation, the nervous system can become overstressed. Phoenix Risers are particularly prone to conditions like chronic fatigue, autoimmune disorders, and other stress-related illnesses because they've spent so long pushing themselves without tending to their deeper needs.

Another challenge for Phoenix Risers is the tendency to rely on their **independence** as a form of protection and their strength as a shield. They've become so adept at rising from the ashes that they may struggle with vulnerability, which they worry may be seen as weakness. They've also become so skilled at surviving on their own that they may struggle to let others in. Asking for help, or even acknowledging their need for support, can reinforce their perception of weakness.

The Phoenix Riser must learn to embrace their vulnerability, to let go of the belief that strength is only found in solitude, and to recognise that healing often comes through connection. Trusting others can feel impossible when we've been burned before and the weight of our past traumas can feel like an anchor dragging us down. After all, it takes incredible strength to acknowledge the pain we're carrying, and sometimes it feels easier to keep moving forward on our own, than it does to sit with the hurt and share the load.

However, true growth comes from allowing ourselves to feel, to heal, and to be vulnerable in our own journey.

Embracing Your Growth as a Phoenix Riser

If you identify with the Phoenix Riser archetype, the key to accelerating your post-traumatic growth lies in embracing both your **strength** and your **vulnerability**.

Yes, you are resilient. Yes, you are powerful. But healing doesn't just come from rising—it needs to also come from resting, reflecting, and allowing yourself to feel the full spectrum of your emotions. I know this might feel scary, especially when you've spent so long relying on your strength, but you've already been through so much worse. Vulnerability will not break you.

One of the most powerful ways Phoenix Risers can facilitate growth is by recognising the importance of **balance**. You don't always have to be in "rising" mode. It's okay to take a step back, to rest in the ashes for a while, and to give yourself permission to heal at your own pace. Your strength isn't diminished by rest—it's enhanced by it. The more you allow yourself to rest, to regulate your nervous system, and process your emotions, the more powerful and sustainable your next rise will be. It is also helpful for you to be prepared to set some boundaries as you give yourself permission to rest. Setting those boundaries protects your energy and keeps burnout at bay.

Embrace your vulnerability and allow yourself to lean on others. The idea of doing so may feel counterintuitive when you've relied for so long on your strength, yet vulnerability is not a sign of weakness, rather a testament to your courage. This doesn't mean giving up your independence, but rather recognising that you don't have to carry everything alone. Allowing yourself to connect with others and share the burden of your journey will lead to more powerful outcomes.

Another key to accelerating your growth as a Phoenix Riser is cultivating **self-compassion**. You've been through so much, and it's important to be gentle with yourself as you continue this journey. You don't have to have it all figured out right away, and it's okay if your progress isn't linear, in fact it rarely will be. Healing is a process, and every step you take—no matter how small—is a victory.

Finally, as a Phoenix Riser you can find strength in your **adaptability** and accelerate your growth by leaning into this adaptability. You've already proven that you can adjust and thrive in new circumstances, so why not use that adaptability to explore new ways of healing? Whether it's through therapy, coaching, mindfulness practices, creative expression, or something entirely different, don't be afraid to try new approaches.

You have the power to transform not just your trauma, but your entire life. Your strength lies in your ability to transform your pain into purpose.

Practical Tools for the Phoenix Riser

Here are some tools and strategies that can help Phoenix Risers continue to grow and heal:

1. **Restorative Practices**: Prioritise rest and nervous system regulation through practices such as meditation, yoga, or deep breathing exercises. These help to calm the body and mind and assist in preventing burnout.

2. **Journalling**: Writing down your thoughts and feelings can help you process emotions and gain clarity on your journey. It also serves as a reminder of how far you've come.

3. **Therapy**: Engaging in some therapy or coaching with someone who understands trauma can be invaluable. Therapists can help you navigate your healing, and coaches can provide structure as you move forward.

4. **Community Support**: Seek out groups or communities where you can connect with others who are also on a similar journey. Support from like-minded individuals can provide both encouragement and a sense of belonging.

5. **Mind-Body Practices**: Explore practices that connect your body and mind, such as TRE (Tension and Trauma Release Exercises), which can help release stored trauma and tension from the body. This is a very powerful process in effective nervous system regulation.

6. **Creative Outlets**: Expressing yourself through art, music, or writing can be incredibly healing. These outlets allow you to process emotions in ways that words alone sometimes cannot.

7. **Self-Compassion Exercises**: Practice self-compassion through exercises like affirmations, gratitude journalling, and gentle self-talk. Remind yourself that you're doing the best you can, and that's enough.

Case Study: Mia's Phoenix Rise

Let me tell you about Mia. Mia came to me after years of battling a traumatic past that included a painful childhood and a series of abusive relationships. When I met her, she was deep in the ashes—feeling lost, overwhelmed, and unsure of how to move forward.

But even in the midst of Mia's pain, I could see the fire inside her: she wasn't prepared to stay down. She had been knocked down so many times, yet she wasn't ready to give up. She had the heart of a Phoenix Riser.

Over the course of our work together, Mia began to rise. She tapped into her resilience, her inner fortitude and found new ways to adapt to her circumstances, then slowly but surely, began to rebuild her life.

What really accelerated her growth was the moment she allowed herself to be vulnerable. For years, she had kept everything hidden from the world, as she didn't want people to see her as 'weak', and she relied on her own strength to carry her through.

It wasn't until Mia allowed herself to feel the depth of her pain that she truly began to heal. Then she discovered how to process her hurt, move through the emotions, and let go of her pain.

Mia's rise wasn't linear—it was a process. There were moments when she had to step back and rest, moments when she felt like she was sinking back into the ashes. But each time, after giving herself permission to rest and regulate her nervous system, she rose again, stronger and more empowered than before.

Today, Mia is thriving. She's using her story to inspire others, and she's a living example of the power of the Phoenix Riser archetype.

Conclusion: The Power of the Phoenix Riser and Soaring Higher

As a Phoenix Riser, your journey has been filled with both pain and triumph. You've faced the fire, and time and again, you've chosen to rise. Now, it's time to take your growth to the next level by embracing the full spectrum of your strength and vulnerability. Healing is not just about rising from the ashes—it's about learning to soar.

You have the power to turn your trauma into triumph. You have an incredible gift for resilience and adaptability, and with each rise, you become stronger, wiser, and more empowered.

Just remember, true growth comes from embracing both your strength and your vulnerability. Give yourself permission to rest, to feel, and to heal at your own pace.

By cultivating balance, allowing yourself to rest, and connecting with others, you can continue to rise higher than you ever thought possible. You are a powerful force of transformation, and your journey of post-traumatic growth is far from over. The next time you feel the flames of your past creeping up, remember that you've risen before, and you will rise again.

Your journey is yours, it's not a race, and there is no right or wrong way to rise.

In the chapters ahead, we'll explore the other Trauma Archetypes and their unique strengths and challenges. But for now, take a moment to honour your own journey as a Phoenix Riser. You are a force of nature, and your story is one of transformation, empowerment, and hope.

CHAPTER 5

The Resilient Sage

-

Wisdom from Wounds

"Turn your wounds into wisdom."

— Oprah Winfrey

The Resilient Sage is the embodiment of wisdom, introspection and of deep understanding—wisdom that has been hard-won and forged in the fires of experience, hardship, and pain. This archetype reflects the individuals who have weathered life's storms and emerged enriched with insights that can guide not only themselves, but others also. The journey of the Resilient Sage is not about merely surviving adversity but about gaining transformative wisdom from these trials and using it as a compass for life.

Unlike the Phoenix Riser, whose strength lies in continually rising from the ashes, the Resilient Sage takes a more reflective, thoughtful approach to healing. The Resilient Sage is someone who dives deep into their experiences, finding meaning in every moment, especially the painful ones.

Their resilience comes not from avoiding challenges, but from facing them head-on, learning and growing with each step.

They have learned to see trauma not just as something to overcome, but as a profound teacher. For the Resilient Sage, trauma becomes a stepping stone—an experience that shapes them, deepens their understanding of life, and gives them the insight needed to guide both themselves and others through the healing process. Their journey is not only personal but also becomes a beacon of light for those seeking guidance through similar challenges.

You will find as you explore each of the archetypes that you will connect with more than one, and that your connection will likely change over the course of your healing journey. Like the Phoenix Riser, the Resilient Sage deeply resonates with me as I've encountered so many Resilient Sages on my journey - individuals who, despite their trauma, possess an incredible depth of insight and can not only see the learnings from their experience, but embrace these lessons as guides that propel them through life's difficulties.

The Resilient Sage knows that life is full of complexities. There are so many moving parts and layers involved. Instead of running from pain, they've learned to sit with it, listen to it, and allow it to inform their choices.

They possess the kind of wisdom that only comes from having walked through the darkest parts of life and come out the other side - albeit not unscathed, but more grounded, more aware, and more compassionate.

The Core Qualities and Strengths of the Resilient Sage

At the heart of the Resilient Sage archetype is wisdom. Not the kind of wisdom that comes from reading books or attending seminars. This is wisdom earned through lived experience, wisdom forged in the crucible of hardship that allows them to make thoughtful decisions, offer compassionate guidance, and find peace in situations that might overwhelm others.

Resilient Sages have faced their trauma head-on and through that process have gained profound insights into themselves, their relationships, and the world around them. They excel in reflection, self-awareness, and the ability to distil life's lessons into wisdom. This wisdom empowers them to take a more measured approach to healing. They're not in a rush to "fix" themselves or move past their trauma. Instead, they understand that healing is a journey, one that requires patience, reflection, and deep introspection. Because of this, they often emanate a calm, grounded presence and a unique perspective that can turn any adversity into an opportunity for learning.

The wisdom of the Resilient Sage gives them a unique ability to approach life's challenges with grace. They have learned to pause, reflect, and consider their options carefully before acting. This ability to see the bigger picture, to take a long-term view of situations, is a powerful asset. It allows them to navigate complex emotional landscapes with ease, turning adversity into opportunity and pain into purpose.

This wisdom and insight make them a natural guide and mentor, whether they realise it or not. They are the confidante, the listener, the one who sees beyond the surface and understands the deeper connections and patterns in life. Their presence alone inspires others to reflect on their own journeys and find meaning in their struggles. They inspire others in so many ways.

Another core strength of the Resilient Sage is their ability to see trauma as a stepping stone rather than a roadblock. Where others might see trauma as something that derails their lives, they see it as an opportunity for growth, learning, and transformation. This doesn't mean that they welcome trauma—far from it—but they find meaning in their suffering, extract the lessons it has to offer, and use those lessons to shape their future in a more intentional, empowered way.

Their resilience lies not in the absence of hardship, but in their capacity to embrace it and grow from it. They've learned to hold space for both their pain and their healing, understanding that they are two sides of the same coin.

The Challenges of the Resilient Sage

While they possess great wisdom and insight, they also face unique challenges on their healing journey. One of the biggest is the tendency to intellectualise their trauma rather than fully feel it. Resilient Sages are so adept at reflecting on their experiences and extracting meaning from them, there may be a tendency to sometimes stay in their head rather than fully engage with their emotions. For true healing to occur, they must learn to balance their intellectual understanding with emotional processing.

This can create a sense of emotional disconnection, where they are aware of their trauma on a cognitive level but struggle to engage with the deeper emotions that still linger beneath the surface. True healing requires them to balance their intellectual understanding with emotional processing. Only by allowing themselves to feel the full spectrum of emotions—grief, anger, sadness, and even joy—can they release the trauma that remains stored in their body and psyche.

Another challenge for the Resilient Sage is overthinking. Their natural tendency toward introspection and analysis, while a strength, can also become a double-edged sword. They may find themselves replaying scenarios in their mind, over-analysing their choices, or second-guessing their decisions. This can lead to what is commonly referred to as "analysis paralysis," where decision-making becomes difficult because of being too focused on weighing the pros and cons of every potential outcome.

This overthinking can also extend to their relationships, where they may find themselves over-analysing interactions or struggling to let go of perceived mistakes. The key to overcoming this challenge is to learn to trust their instincts and to embrace the uncertainty of life. They don't need to have everything figured out all the time—sometimes, the best course of action is simply to take the next step, trusting that they will learn and grow along the way.

Isolation is another potential pitfall for the Resilient Sage. Their natural inclination toward introspection may lead them to retreat into their inner world where they feel more comfortable, disconnecting from others. This can lead to feelings of loneliness or emotional distance, where they can become a detached observer of their own life rather than an active participant in it. While solitude can be a valuable tool for self-reflection, it's important to recognise when it becomes a barrier to connection.

The challenge here is to strike a balance between solitude and connection. It's important to remember that they don't have to carry the weight of their trauma alone. Reaching out to others for support, whether through friendships, therapy, or community, is an important step in their healing journey.

Finally, the weight of their wisdom can sometimes feel like a burden. The Resilient Sage may feel responsible for guiding others through their healing journeys, even at the expense of their own well-being. Their natural inclination to offer support and advice to those around them means Resilient Sages often take on the role of mentor or guide. While this is a beautiful expression of their archetype, it can also lead to burnout if they neglect their own needs in the process.

Embracing Your Growth as a Resilient Sage

If you identify with the Resilient Sage archetype, the key to accelerating your post-traumatic growth lies in striking a balance between introspection and action.

You've already mastered the art of reflection and insight—now it's time to bring those insights into your emotional world. This will mean allowing yourself to feel the full range of emotions that come with trauma, even the ones that you find uncomfortable or difficult to sit with.

One powerful way to facilitate this growth is through mindfulness practices that bring you out of your head and into your body. Mindfulness practices ground you in the present moment, reducing the urge to dwell on past mistakes or future uncertainties.

Doing practices like meditation, yoga, or breathwork can help you to stay present with your emotions rather than intellectualising them. These practices serve to create a space for you to fully feel and process your emotions in a safe, and grounded way. Mindfulness also helps you cultivate a sense of compassion toward yourself, recognising that healing is not a linear process. You don't have to have all the answers, and it's okay to allow yourself to be vulnerable.

Another way you can accelerate your growth as a Resilient Sage is by embracing your vulnerability. It is important to recognise that you don't have to have all the answers all the time. It's okay to admit that you're still figuring things out, and it's okay to lean on others for support. True wisdom doesn't come from pretending to have it all together! It comes from us acknowledging the full spectrum of our experience, including the parts that are not yet resolved or understood.

Finally, you can enhance your growth by giving yourself permission to put your own healing first. You have so much to offer others, and you need to remember that your well-being matters too. It is totally okay to take a step back from guiding others and focus on your own journey. In fact, the more you prioritise your own healing, the more you'll be able to offer those around you.

Case Study: Davina's Sage-like Wisdom

Let me introduce you to Davina, a true Resilient Sage. Davina had experienced significant trauma throughout her life, including the loss of her parents at a young age in a car accident and a series of painful personal relationships.

When I met her, she was incredibly insightful, able to articulate the many lessons she had learned from her trauma with clarity and depth. But there was something missing—I noticed an emotional disconnect that left her feeling stuck in her healing journey.

During our work together, Davina began to realise that while she understood her trauma on a cognitive level, she hadn't given herself permission to fully feel the pain and grief that still lingered beneath the surface. She was afraid that if she opened the floodgates to her emotions, she would be overwhelmed and unable to cope.

To help Davina reconnect with her emotions, we incorporated mindfulness practices into her healing journey. She began meditating regularly, using breathwork to ground herself in the present moment. Slowly but surely, she began to feel safe enough to explore her emotions—first in small doses, and then more fully as she grew more comfortable with the process.

Through mindfulness practices and then emotional processing, and some coaching, Davina began to reconnect with her emotions. She allowed herself to grieve, to feel the sadness, anger, and hurt that she had long kept at arm's length to maintain her own sense of safety.

Over time, Davina began to release the pain that had been stored in her body for years. She cried for the first time in many months, allowing herself to grieve for the losses she had experienced. She also began to express her emotions more openly in her relationships, no longer feeling the need to hide behind her intellect or wisdom.

As Davina embraced her emotional world, processed her stored emotions and released her years of pain and hurt she found that her own wisdom deepened. She was no longer just reflecting on her trauma and analysing it—she was fully engaging with it, feeling it, and allowing it to inform her choices in a more holistic and healthy way.

Davina's journey as a Resilient Sage was one of balancing her natural insight with her emotional vulnerability. By allowing herself to feel the full spectrum of her emotions, she was able to release the trauma that had been holding her back and step into a new chapter of her life with greater clarity and peace.

Today, Davina continues to share her wisdom with others, and she does so from a place of deep emotional connection. She is not just guiding others from her head—she's guiding them from her heart.

Conclusion: The Power of the Resilient Sage and the Wisdom Within

As a Resilient Sage, your journey is one of deep wisdom and profound insight. You have the unique ability to find meaning in your trauma, transforming your pain into purpose and turning your trauma into wisdom. You see your experiences not as obstacles, but as opportunities for significant growth. Your insights, reflection, and calm presence make you a powerful guide for both yourself and for others.

However, it's important to remember that true wisdom comes from balancing your intellectual understanding with emotional engagement and engaging in emotional processing and vulnerability. Give yourself permission to feel, to be vulnerable, and to prioritise your own healing.

By balancing your natural tendency toward introspection with practices that help you connect with your emotions, you can accelerate your growth and move more fully into the post-traumatic growth phase. Embrace your wisdom, but don't be afraid to feel the emotions that come with it. In doing so, you will continue to evolve, not just as a survivor of trauma, but as a true Resilient Sage.

In the chapters to come, we'll explore the other Trauma Archetypes and their unique paths to post-traumatic growth. But for now, take a moment to honour your own journey as a Resilient Sage. You've already come so far, and your wisdom will continue to light the way as you move forward.

CHAPTER 6

The Empowered Trailblazer

Forging New Paths

"Do not go where the path may lead, go instead where there is no path and leave a trail."

— Ralph Waldo Emerson

The Empowered Trailblazer is a force to be reckoned with. They are natural leaders who, after experiencing trauma, emerge stronger, braver, and more determined than ever to carve out new paths for themselves and for others.

Where some may retreat into themselves after adversity, the Empowered Trailblazer chooses to step forward, breaking through barriers and pushing past limits with a sense of purpose and courage. This archetype is all about taking action, making bold moves, and creating change – not just for themselves, but for the world around them.

An Empowered Trailblazer's beauty lies in their ability to transform pain into power. They've undoubtedly endured hardship, but instead of letting it define them, they use it as fuel to light the way forward. They're the ones who refuse to let trauma keep them down. Instead, they rise, they lead, and they inspire others to do the same.

There's a fire in their heart – a relentless drive to not just survive but to thrive, to overcome adversity, and to pave the way for others to follow.

The Core Qualities of the Empowered Trailblazer

At the core of the Empowered Trailblazer is **courage**. These individuals have faced some of the darkest moments imaginable, and yet they emerge with an unshakeable determination to move forward, almost as if what they've endured has strengthened their resolve.

This courage isn't just about bravery in the face of danger; it's about the inner strength and fortitude to keep going even when the road ahead is uncertain and filled with obstacles. Empowered Trailblazers are willing to step into the unknown, take risks, and trust in their innate ability to navigate whatever comes their way.

Another defining quality of the Empowered Trailblazer is their **leadership**. These individuals are not content to follow the status quo – they're driven to create new paths and inspire others to follow them. Whether it's in their personal lives, their careers, or their communities, Empowered Trailblazers are often seen as visionaries. They're the ones who see possibilities where others see roadblocks, and they have the courage to lead the charge.

Empowered Trailblazers are also deeply driven by **purpose**. Their trauma has often ignited within them a sense of mission and grand vision – a desire to make a meaningful impact on the world. This might manifest as a commitment to helping others heal, advocating for social change, or pursuing a personal dream with fierce determination. Whatever the form, Empowered

Trailblazers are propelled by a deep sense of purpose that gives their lives meaning and direction and moves them forward.

This sense of purpose is often born from a personal transformation—a realisation that life after trauma can have greater meaning than it did before. Empowered Trailblazers harness the lessons learned from their experiences and infuse them into everything they do. They become trailblazers not just by accident, but by the deep calling to create a legacy that matters.

The Challenges of the Empowered Trailblazer

While the Empowered Trailblazer's drive and courage are their greatest strengths, they can also present unique challenges.

One of the most common challenges for this archetype is burnout. Empowered Trailblazers are often so focused on moving forward and leading others that they tend to forget to take care of themselves along the way. They push themselves to the limit, constantly striving to achieve more and make a bigger impact. But this relentless drive can lead to exhaustion, both physically and emotionally. Over time, the burden of leadership and the constant pursuit of success without rest can lead to a depletion of energy and motivation.

Burnout can manifest in various ways: a lack of joy in activities that once brought them satisfaction, difficulty sleeping or concentrating, and emotional detachment from loved ones or from their purpose. Trailblazers are known for their endurance, but they must also recognise that endurance without rest is unsustainable. Taking a step back to recharge is not a sign of weakness but rather an acknowledgment of their humanity.

Another challenge for Empowered Trailblazers is the tendency to **over commit**. Their desire to create change and forge new paths can sometimes lead them to over-extend themselves, taking on more responsibilities and commitments than they can realistically handle. This can result in them feeling overwhelmed, stressed, and even discouraged when they're unable to handle everything they set out to do. Making and holding boundaries can be a challenge for them.

Often, the Empowered Trailblazer wants to be everything for everyone—to save the world, help every person, and tackle every challenge. However, overextending themselves can result in them neglecting their own needs and ultimately diminishing their impact. As much as they want to push forward, they must learn the art of saying "no" and prioritising what truly aligns with their purpose.

Finally, Empowered Trailblazers may struggle with **vulnerability**. Because they're often seen as strong, capable leaders, they may feel pressure to always have it together. This can make it difficult for them to ask for help or to admit to others when they are struggling. Yet true empowerment comes from embracing both strength and vulnerability and learning to lean on others when needed.

Many Trailblazers believe that they must shoulder the burden of their path alone. However, the greatest leaders understand that they are stronger when supported by a community. Vulnerability doesn't mean weakness—it means allowing others to witness your humanity and to share the load. By embracing their vulnerability, Trailblazers allow space for others to grow alongside them, fostering a more authentic and resilient form of leadership.

Embracing Growth as an Empowered Trailblazer

If you feel you could be an Empowered Trailblazer, then the key to accelerating your post-traumatic growth lies in finding a balance between action and self-care. You have an incredible drive and determination, but it's important to remember that rest and rejuvenation are just as essential to your growth as taking action.

Self-care isn't a sign of weakness – it's a necessary part of sustaining your energy and resilience for the long haul. By nurturing yourself and honouring your desire to bring your mission to life, you need to focus on achieving this balance. This could mean scheduling regular time off, engaging in practices that replenish your energy, or seeking out mentors and supporters who can guide you along your journey.

One powerful way to support your growth is by **setting clear boundaries** around your time and your energy. As an Empowered

Trailblazer, you're likely passionate about many things, but you simply can't do it all. Prioritise the activities and causes that truly align with your purpose and give yourself permission to say no to the rest. This will help you stay focused on what matters most and prevent burnout, whilst helping you to forge your path in the process.

Boundaries also mean protecting your emotional and mental space. Not every battle is yours to fight, and not every problem is yours to solve. Recognising where your energy is best spent will allow you to channel your efforts into the areas where you can have the most impact.

Another way to enhance your growth is by embracing your **vulnerability**. Leadership isn't about always having the answers or being perfect – it's about being authentic and being human. Allow yourself to be open about your challenges, and don't be afraid to lean on others for support. By showing your vulnerability, you'll not only strengthen your resilience, but you'll also inspire those around you to do the same.

Vulnerability also allows for deeper connections with those you lead. When you're willing to share your struggles, you create an environment of trust and openness that encourages others to bring their authentic selves to the table. In this way, your vulnerability becomes a powerful tool for collective growth.

Tools and Strategies for the Empowered Trailblazer

To truly thrive as an Empowered Trailblazer, consider incorporating the following tools and strategies into your life:

1. **Mindful Reflection:** Take time to reflect on your journey regularly. Journalling can a useful tool to help you process emotions, track your progress, and maintain clarity on your goals. Reflection allows you to stay grounded in your purpose and make adjustments along the way.

2. **Mentorship and Support Systems:** Surround yourself with mentors and like-minded individuals who understand your mission and can offer guidance as and when required. Lean on them during challenging times and seek their wisdom to help you navigate your path with greater clarity.

3. **Restorative Practices:** Engage in practices that restore your energy, such as yoga, meditation, or walks in nature. These practices can help you recharge and stay balanced as you continue to lead and inspire others.

4. **Delegate and Collaborate:** Empower others by delegating responsibilities and collaborating on projects. This not only lightens your load but also fosters growth in those around you, and enhances your leadership, creating a ripple effect of positive change.

5. **Celebrate Small Wins:** Acknowledge and celebrate the small victories along your journey. This will help you

maintain momentum and remind you of the progress you've made, even when the road ahead feels long.

Case Study: Sarah's Trailblazing Journey

Sarah is the epitome of an Empowered Trailblazer. After surviving a devastating car accident, she felt a strong pull to use her experience to help others. She became a passionate advocate for road safety, launching a campaign to raise awareness about the dangers of distracted driving. Sarah's courage and leadership quickly gained attention, and she found herself at the forefront of a movement that was saving lives.

But as Sarah's campaign grew, so did her responsibilities. She was constantly on the go – organising events, speaking at schools, and managing a growing team of volunteers as she increased her reach. Eventually, Sarah began to feel the effects of burnout. She was exhausted, emotionally drained and struggling to keep up with the demands of her role. She felt torn between her mission and the need for taking care of herself.

Recognising the need for balance, Sarah made a conscious decision to scale back her commitments, slow down and focus on what mattered most and prioritise her well-being. She started delegating tasks to her team, set boundaries around her time, and work, incorporated regular self-care practices like yoga and meditation into her routine.

By finding a balance between action and rest, Sarah was able to sustain her energy and continue leading with passion and purpose. As a result, things gradually improved and Sarah was able to continue leading her campaign with renewed energy and focus. By taking care of herself, she became an even stronger leader, her impact expanded, and her mission became a reality.

Through her vulnerability, Sarah connected more deeply with her team and her audience, fostering a sense of community that made her movement even more impactful. Today, Sarah continues to forge new paths, creating lasting change while staying grounded in her self-care and sense of purpose.

Conclusion: The Power of the Empowered Trailblazer

The Empowered Trailblazer is a symbol of strength, courage, and vision. By leading with purpose, embracing vulnerability, and balancing action with self-care, you have the potential to create profound change not just in your own life, but in the lives of those around you.

As an Empowered Trailblazer, you possess the incredible ability to turn adversity into action, to lead with courage and determination and to create meaningful change in the world. Your resilience, leadership, and purpose-driven mindset make you a powerful force for good.

But remember, true empowerment comes from you finding the balance. Take care of yourself as fiercely as you take care of others, and don't be afraid to embrace vulnerability as part of your journey. As you continue your journey, remember that leadership is not about perfection—it's about authenticity, growth, and a relentless drive to forge a better path.

In the next chapter, we'll explore another archetype with a different yet equally powerful approach to post-traumatic growth. For now, honour your trailblazing spirit and trust that you have the strength and the wisdom to continue forging paths – both for yourself and for those who follow in your footsteps.

CHAPTER 7

The Reflective Orchestrator

—

Healing Through Reflection

"Life can only be understood backwards; but it must be lived forwards."

— **Søren Kierkegaard**

The Reflective Orchestrator is the wise, deliberate planner who approaches post-traumatic growth with a sense of calm, patience, and keen observation. After enduring trauma, they step into a space of thoughtful reflection, seeking to understand the bigger picture and create a healing process that is both meaningful and sustainable in the longer term. Where some may rush through their healing journey, the Reflective Orchestrator takes time to consider each step carefully, ensuring that every move they make is in alignment with their deeper self.

This archetype is characterised by its strategic thinking and ability to pause, reflect and plan. Reflective Orchestrators are known for their patience and commitment to understanding not just their trauma, but themselves. They find healing by orchestrating their internal and external worlds in a way that promotes harmony, growth and clarity. Their path to recovery is not about rushing or forcing themselves forward – it's about gently guiding themselves through a process of self-discovery and emotional balance.

The Reflective Orchestrator is the planner, the organiser, the one who finds comfort in structure and creating order out of chaos. Even in the aftermath of trauma, where emotions may feel overwhelming or disorienting, the Reflective Orchestrator maintains a focus on establishing coherence in their environment and inner world. They thrive on a sense of control, not in an unhealthy way, but rather in their ability to bring structure to the unstructured. Their ability to weave together their insights and reflections forms the foundation of their healing journey. They are excellent at managing their environment and finding ways to make things work, even in the face of adversity.

The Core Qualities of the Reflective Orchestrator

One of the most defining qualities of the Reflective Orchestrator is their gift for **deep introspection**. After trauma, Reflective Orchestrators don't shy away from their emotions; instead, they dive into them with a sense of curiosity and a desire to understand their full impact. They have an innate ability to look inward and gain insight from their experiences, using those insights to guide their healing journey with wisdom and care. This introspective ability allows them to explore their feelings, reactions, and beliefs about their trauma, ultimately transforming those emotions into catalysts for personal growth.

Reflective Orchestrators are also **highly patient**. They recognise that healing from trauma is not a quick or linear process and is more often a winding path with peaks and troughs. They're willing to give themselves the time and space needed to heal fully. This patience allows them to move through their recovery with grace, trusting that each moment of reflection brings them closer to a deeper understanding of themselves and clarity for their path forward. Unlike those who might seek quick fixes, the Reflective Orchestrator knows that lasting healing is a long-term commitment.

Strategic thinking is another hallmark of the Reflective Orchestrator. These individuals are skilled at organising their thoughts, emotions, and experiences into a coherent plan for healing. They don't just react to their trauma, they respond to it with a sense of purpose and intentionality. By creating a clear vision of their healing process, they can move forward with a sense of direction and confidence, knowing that every step they take is aligned with their long-term wellbeing in the direction of post-traumatic growth. The Reflective Orchestrator is always thinking about the big picture, even as they focus on the smaller steps needed to achieve their goals.

Another core quality is **emotional resilience**. While some may avoid confronting their trauma, Reflective Orchestrators know that healing involves embracing their pain, not running from it. They approach their emotional landscape with the same strategic mindset they apply to other aspects of their lives. They assess their emotions, work through them methodically, and use their insights to strengthen their ability to face future challenges. This resilience allows them to maintain emotional balance, even when revisiting painful memories or confronting difficult emotions. By cultivating this resilience, they turn their vulnerability into a source of strength.

The Challenges of the Reflective Orchestrator

While the Reflective Orchestrator's ability to pause and reflect is a tremendous strength, it can also present challenges. One of the most common challenges for this archetype is the tendency to overthink. Reflective Orchestrators can sometimes get caught in a cycle of 'analysis paralysis' where they spend so much time reflecting on their trauma and planning their next steps that they struggle to take clear action. This can lead to feelings of frustration at being stuck or unable to move forward, despite their deep desire for growth. Overthinking can also fuel self-doubt, making it difficult to trust their instincts or believe that they are making the right decisions.

Another challenge for Reflective Orchestrators is the risk of becoming too isolated. Because they spend so much time in their own heads, Reflective Orchestrators may withdraw from the world around them, feeling more comfortable in their own thoughts than in the presence of others. While solitude can be a valuable part of the healing process, too much isolation can hinder their ability to connect with others and receive the support they need. It's important for Reflective Orchestrators to remember that healing is not something that can be done entirely alone. Connecting with others provides a valuable opportunity to gain perspective, share insights, and receive guidance from those who have walked similar paths.

Finally, Reflective Orchestrators may struggle with balancing their emotions. Their deep introspection can sometimes lead them to dwell on negative emotions or relive painful experiences without finding the resolution they desire. While reflecting on trauma is an important part of the healing process, it's equally important to find closure and move forward. Reflective Orchestrators can sometimes become stuck in the past, unable to fully release their emotional burdens.

A challenge here for a Reflective Orchestrator is to not become too rigid or controlling as a way of managing their fears. This can create an emotional imbalance that makes it difficult to move forward with clarity and peace. They must learn to balance introspection with self-compassion and emotional release.

This tendency toward control can also manifest in perfectionism. Reflective Orchestrators may feel compelled to "perfect" their healing journey, carefully orchestrating every step to ensure that they don't make mistakes or experience setbacks. While planning and structure are helpful, the need for perfection can become a barrier to growth. Healing is inherently messy and unpredictable, and Reflective Orchestrators must learn to embrace the imperfections of their journey. Letting go of the need for control and allowing themselves to be vulnerable can be difficult, but it is an essential part of the process.

Exercises for Building Self-Awareness and Emotional Balance

For Reflective Orchestrators, one of the most important aspects of their healing journey is building self-awareness. Increasing their self-awareness allows them to better understand their emotional landscape and recognise when they are caught up in patterns of over-thinking or emotional overwhelm. With greater awareness, they can make conscious choices about how to respond to their emotions, rather than reacting out of fear or anxiety.

1. **Reflective Journalling:** An exercise that can help with this is to maintain a reflective journal. By regularly writing down their thoughts and emotions Reflective Orchestrators can gain clarity on their inner world and track their progress over time. Journalling allows them to externalise their thoughts, creating a sense of order and coherence. It also provides a space for them to process difficult emotions, celebrate small victories, and identify patterns in their thinking. For Reflective Orchestrators, journalling can be a powerful tool for grounding themselves and creating emotional balance.

2. **Mindfulness Meditation:** Mindfulness helps a Reflective Orchestrator to stay present in the moment, preventing them from getting lost in their thoughts or emotions. By cultivating a sense of mindful awareness, they can observe their feelings without becoming overwhelmed by them, allowing them to find greater emotional balance and peace. Mindfulness also helps Reflective Orchestrators practice non-judgmental self-awareness, which is key to overcoming perfectionism and self-criticism. Regular mindfulness practice can help them to stay grounded in the present moment and reduce their tendency to overthink.

3. **Creating a Structured Plan:** Reflective Orchestrators can benefit from creating a structured plan for their healing journey. This might involve setting specific goals for their recovery, identifying the steps they need to take to achieve those goals, and creating a timeline for when they hope to reach each milestone. By organising their thoughts and emotions into a clear plan, a Reflective Orchestrator can feel more empowered and focused as they move through the healing process.

4. **Increasing Flexibility:** Flexibility is key as life doesn't always go according to plan...and that's okay. Learning to adapt to changes and letting go of control in small ways will build their resilience and help them avoid becoming rigid or frustrated when things don't go as expected.

5. **Emotional Release:** This might involve activities such as art therapy, where they can express their emotions in a creative and non-verbal way, or body-based practices such as yoga or TRE (Tension & Trauma Releasing Exercises), which can help release stored tension and trauma from the body. These practices allow them to move beyond intellectual understanding and engage with their emotions on a deeper, and more intuitive level.

Embracing Growth as a Reflective Orchestrator

If you feel you could be a Reflective Orchestrator, then the key to accelerating your post-traumatic growth lies in finding balance between reflection and taking action.

As a Reflective Orchestrator, your ability to reflect deeply and think strategically is a powerful tool in your healing journey. You have a natural gift for understanding yourself and your emotions, and this self-awareness can guide you through the complexities of post-traumatic growth. However, remember that growth also requires action. Don't let yourself get stuck in the planning phase – take those insights you've gained and put them into practice.

To further enhance your growth, focus on finding balance between reflection and action. Give 0yourself permission to take small, yet intentional steps forward, even if you don't have everything figured out just yet. Healing doesn't need to be perfect—it's okay to make mistakes or feel uncertain along the way. Trust that your strategic mindset and emotional resilience will carry you through any challenges you encounter. Trust that you really don't need to have all the answers before you can move forward – you can refine your path as you go.

At the same time, make space for emotional release. Allow yourself to feel your emotions fully, without trying to control or manage them. Letting go of the need to orchestrate every aspect of your healing will create more room for growth, freedom, and emotional healing.

By integrating your strengths of introspection and strategic thinking with the ability to embrace vulnerability and act, you will experience profound growth and transformation. You have the tools you need to heal and thrive, and your journey as a Reflective Orchestrator will continue to unfold as you navigate your way toward greater emotional balance, self-awareness, and post-traumatic growth.

Another important aspect of your growth is connecting with others. Whilst introspection is valuable, it's equally important to reach out for support and engage with the world around you. Sharing your insights and experiences with others can help you gain new perspectives and strengthen your sense of connection with both self and others.

Case Study: Jane's Orchestrated Healing

Jane embodies the Reflective Orchestrator archetype. After experiencing a sudden and highly traumatic loss, Jane found herself retreating into her own world of introspection with her thoughts going over and over in her head. She spent countless hours reflecting on the events that had unfolded, trying to make sense of her emotions and the impact the trauma and the loss had on her life. Jane's patience allowed her to process her grief slowly and thoughtfully, however she eventually realised that her introspection had become a form of avoidance.

Recognising the need for balance, Jane began incorporating mindfulness meditation and time walking in nature into her daily routine. This practice assisted her to stay grounded in the present moment, preventing her from getting so lost in her thoughts and allowed her that deeper level of emotional connection to herself. She also started journalling, which allowed her to organise her thoughts and her emotions and to gain a clearer understanding of the way forward for her healing process. By combining her natural gift for reflection with mindfulness and self-awareness, Jane was able to move forward in her healing journey with greater clarity and emotional balance.

Conclusion: The Reflective Orchestrator's Path to Healing

The Reflective Orchestrator's journey is one of thoughtful reflection, strategic planning, and emotional balance. Your ability to pause, reflect, and to plan allows you to navigate your healing process with innate wisdom and clarity. But don't forget to balance that reflection with action and connection.

You have an innate capacity for planning, organising and finding comfort in structure, so increasing your self-awareness and accessing these strengths will allow you to better understand your emotional landscape and recognise when you are caught in over-thinking or emotional overwhelm.

By embracing both introspection and forward movement, whilst building this self-awareness and cultivating emotional balance you can accelerate your post-traumatic growth and create a life that is aligned with your deepest values and desires.

In the next chapter, we'll explore another archetype with a unique approach to post traumatic growth. For now, honour your gift for reflection, and challenge yourself to act. Trust that your thoughtful planning has prepared you well for the next steps on your healing journey.

CHAPTER 8

The Authentic Warrior
-
Strength in Vulnerability

"Vulnerability is not winning or losing; it's having the courage to show up and be seen."

- Brené Brown

The Authentic Warrior is a fierce and courageous archetype, someone who has walked through the fire of trauma and emerged with an unyielding commitment to living in alignment with their truth.

This archetype carries the strength of someone who has faced hardship and chosen not just to survive, but to thrive. They have an inner strength that refuses to be broken, and the Authentic Warrior stands tall in the face of adversity, defending their values and beliefs with determination. The Authentic Warrior is the fierce protector of truth, both for themselves and for those they love.

Authentic Warriors are courageous, determined, and deeply committed to living authentically. They stand up for what they believe in, even when it's hard, and are not afraid to face the difficult aspects of their past or present. However, what sets them apart from the stereotypical image of a warrior is their deep desire to live authentically, embracing both their strength and their vulnerability as integral parts of their journey.

The Authentic Warrior doesn't just fight for survival—they fight for a life that is true to their core, one that honours who they are and what they've been through. They reject the idea of living behind a mask or wearing armour to shield their true selves. Instead, they seek to live with the utmost integrity in all they do, embracing their scars not as weaknesses, but as symbols of their resilience and survival.

At the heart of this archetype is an unwavering commitment to authenticity, a willingness to show up fully as themselves, without pretence or shame even when the world expects them to hide behind armour.

The Core Qualities of the Authentic Warrior

One of the Authentic Warrior's greatest strengths is their ability to stand in their truth, no matter the circumstances. This archetype has an unshakable belief in their values and a commitment to living in alignment with those values, even when it's difficult. They are deeply connected to their inner sense of right and wrong and social justice and are willing to fight for what they believe in, regardless of external pressures. Whether facing societal expectations, interpersonal conflicts, or their internal fears, the Authentic Warrior remains rooted in their core beliefs, refusing to compromise their authenticity for the sake of convenience or acceptance.

The Authentic Warrior is direct, fearless, and deeply loyal. They fight for what they believe in and inspire others to do the same. They are not afraid of conflict because they know that facing it is necessary for growth. Their ability to be real, even when it's uncomfortable, makes them a powerful force in any situation.

Authentic Warriors are also defined by their inner strength. This strength is not just physical nor is it just external—it's a deep, internal resolve that allows them to face challenges head-on. They possess a remarkable ability to confront life's hardships head-on, drawing from a well of resilience that goes beyond the physical or superficial. Even after enduring significant trauma, they have a remarkable ability to keep moving forward, driven by an inner fire that once alight, refuses to be extinguished. This strength propels them forward, often inspires others and serves as a powerful reminder that healing is not just about surviving—it's about thriving in alignment with who they truly are. This resolve is often a beacon of hope and inspiration for others who are navigating their own healing journeys.

Perhaps the most profound quality of the Authentic Warrior is their dedication to authenticity. Unlike the traditional warrior who hides behind armour, and a façade of invincibility, the Authentic Warrior recognises that true strength is found in vulnerability and understands the importance of embracing their vulnerability.

To the Authentic Warrior, true strength lies not in pretending to be invincible, but in being willing to show their complete selves, scars and all. They fight for their truth, but they also know when to soften, when to let others in, and when to allow themselves to be seen in their entirety. By showing their true selves, they encourage others to do the same, creating deeper, more authentic connections in the process.

The Challenges of the Authentic Warrior

Despite their incredible strength and commitment to authenticity, the Authentic Warrior faces unique challenges in their journey to healing. The very qualities that make them resilient can also become stumbling blocks if they are not mindful of how they wield their power. One of the most common struggles for this archetype, is the tendency to over-rely on their strength, to the point where they build walls around themselves to protect their vulnerability. In the face of trauma, this strength has been their shield, allowing them to persevere and to protect themselves from further harm.

Authentic Warriors are often fiercely independent, which has helped them stand strong in the face of adversity. While this survival mechanism has allowed them to navigate the complexities of trauma on their own terms, it can also lead to isolation. Authentic Warriors may resist asking for help or allowing others to support them, believing that they must always be strong and self-reliant. This can leave them feeling disconnected and alone and they may in turn miss out on experiencing the profound healing power that comes from connection and community.

The walls they've built around themselves may actually serve to prevent them from fully experiencing the healing that comes from opening up to others. While their strength has ultimately served them well in surviving trauma, it can also manifest as an inability to soften or show vulnerability and become a barrier to true, deeper healing if they are unwilling to let down their guard and embrace the softer aspects of their humanity.

Another challenge for the Authentic Warrior is the struggle with perfectionism. Their commitment to living authentically can sometimes manifest as an 'all-or-nothing' mentality, where they feel pressured to always be perfectly aligned with their truth and true to themselves in a way that leaves no room for mistakes or imperfections. This can create internal conflict, as they may feel like they are constantly falling short of their own high standards. Learning to embrace imperfection and accept themselves as they are—flaws and all—is an important part of the Authentic Warrior's healing journey.

Learning to Soften the Armour and Embrace Vulnerability

One of the most important transformative lessons for the Authentic Warrior is learning to soften their armour and embrace vulnerability as a source of strength. This can be a challenging process, as it requires them to shift their understanding of what it means to be strong, and to let go of the idea that strength means being invulnerable. Instead, it's about having the courage to be seen, even in moments of fear or uncertainty. They must learn that true strength comes from being able to show up authentically, even when it feels uncomfortable or scary.

One exercise that can help Authentic Warriors soften their armour is practicing self-compassion. It involves offering themselves the same kindness and understanding that they would extend to a close friend. By offering kindness and understanding to themselves, they can begin to dismantle the walls they've built around their hearts. This might involve acknowledging their own pain, validating their emotions, and allowing themselves to feel without self-judgment. Self-compassion teaches the Authentic Warrior that they don't always have to be strong—they can be human, too.

Another powerful practice for Authentic Warriors is cultivating deep, meaningful connections with others. Vulnerability often comes most easily in the context of safe trusted relationships, where they can slowly open up, and allow others to see their true selves. Authentic Warriors can benefit from identifying a few key individuals with whom they feel comfortable sharing their struggles, fears, and insecurities. These relationships provide the space for the Authentic Warrior to be seen in their entirety. By allowing themselves to be vulnerable in these relationships, they can experience the profound healing that comes from being truly understood and accepted.

Finally, Authentic Warriors can benefit from creating rituals of self-reflection and grounding. Taking time to reflect on their journey and reconnect with their authentic self can help them stay centred and aligned with their true values. This might involve journalling, meditating, or spending time in nature—whatever helps them feel rooted in their truth. By grounding themselves regularly through the rituals they create, they can release the need for constant vigilance and trust in their own resilience.

The Strength of Connection: Building a Support System

As an Authentic Warrior, one of the most important elements of healing is learning to accept support from others. While independence has been a key part of their survival, true growth requires connection. Building a support system of trusted individuals allows the Authentic Warrior to share the burden of healing and experience the transformative power of vulnerability.

To build this support system, the Authentic Warrior can start by:

- Identifying some key individuals who have proven themselves to be trustworthy and supportive.

- Practicing small acts of vulnerability, such as sharing personal struggles or asking for help.

- Creating clear boundaries to ensure that these relationships are rooted in mutual respect and understanding.

By allowing others to see them and to support them, the Authentic Warrior can experience a greater sense of connection and healing at a deeper level.

Embracing Growth as an Authentic Warrior

If you feel you could be an Authentic Warrior, then the key to accelerating your path to post traumatic growth lies in balancing your incredible strength with the courage to be vulnerable. You have a deep commitment to living in alignment with your truth, and that truth includes both your strength and your softness. By learning to soften your armour and embrace vulnerability, you can access a deeper level of healing and growth.

One of the most empowering actions you can take is to allow yourself to be seen. Share your truth with others, not just the parts of yourself that feel strong and resilient, but also the parts that feel tender and raw. By embracing vulnerability, you give yourself permission to be fully human, and you invite others to do the same.

Another key to your growth is recognising that you don't have to do it all on your own. You are incredibly strong, yet true strength also lies in knowing when to ask for help and when to lean on others for support. Allow yourself to experience the healing power of connection, knowing that you don't have to carry the weight of your trauma alone.

Regularly take time to reflect on your journey and reconnect with your authentic self. Journalling, meditating, or spending time in nature can help you stay grounded and centred in your truth.

Case Study: Margaret's Journey to Authenticity

Margaret is the epitome of the Authentic Warrior. After enduring years of emotional abuse, she emerged from her trauma determined to reclaim her life and live in alignment with her truth. For years, she had relied on her inner strength to get through the darkest moments, actively building a fortress around herself to protect her heart and her vulnerability.

However, as Margaret began her healing journey, she realised that her strength alone was not enough, she felt as though something was keeping her 'stuck' and she was unable to move forward despite all her efforts. She recognised that she needed to learn how to embrace her vulnerability if she was going to fully heal.

Margaret's turning point came when she started working with a trauma-informed therapist who encouraged her to explore the parts of herself that she had kept hidden for so long.

Through this work, Margaret was able to accept herself for who she was, and learned that vulnerability was not a weakness, but was actually a source of immense power. She began to soften her armour, allowing herself to feel her emotions and gradually let one or two people in so she could share her struggles with others. As she embraced her vulnerability, Margaret discovered a new depth of strength—one that was rooted in authenticity, connection, and self-compassion.

Margaret's story demonstrates that the path to healing for the Authentic Warrior is not about abandoning strength, but about blending and enhancing it with vulnerability. By allowing herself to be seen in her entirety, Margaret was able to unlock a deeper level of healing and personal growth. As a result, she has made huge progress and now prides herself on opening her heart to others and living her values and inspiring others to do the same.

Conclusion: The Authentic Warrior's Path to Healing

Your journey as an Authentic Warrior is one of strength, courage, integrity and authenticity. You have a remarkable ability to stand in your truth and fight for what you believe in, but your healing requires more than just your strength—it requires vulnerability. By softening your armour and embracing your whole self, you can unlock a new level of healing and growth.

As an Authentic Warrior, you have the courage to live in alignment with your values, even in the face of adversity. Your resilience is undeniable, but so is your capacity for vulnerability. By embracing both, you unlock the power to heal, grow, and thrive.

As you continue your journey, remember that your vulnerability is not a weakness—it is a source of power. Trust in your resilience, but also trust in your ability to be vulnerable and open. In so doing, you will find that your path to post-traumatic growth is not just about surviving, it's about thriving in alignment with your truest self.

In the next chapter, we will explore another archetype with its own unique approach to healing. For now, honour your strength, yet don't be afraid to soften. Allow yourself to be seen, to connect, and to embrace the fullness of who you are.

CHAPTER 9

The Radiant Alchemist - Transforming Pain into Purpose

"*The most beautiful people we have known are those who have known defeat, known suffering, known struggle, known loss, and have found their way out of the depths.*"

– **Elisabeth Kübler-Ross**

The Radiant Alchemist archetype represents one of the most powerful and mystical forces of transformation in the journey from trauma to post-traumatic growth. Those who resonate with the Radiant Alchemist have a rare and extraordinary gift: the ability to transmute their pain into something meaningful, purposeful, and often even profoundly beautiful. Just like an alchemist turns base metals into gold, the Radiant Alchemist has the unique ability to transform their darkness into light, drawing on inner strength and finding hope, healing, and purpose in the process.

The Radiant Alchemist understands that trauma, while painful, is not merely an experience to endure, it can also be a catalyst for profound personal growth and self-reinvention. They do not shy away from the intensity of their emotions; instead, where others may see only suffering, the Radiant Alchemist harnesses that energy and sees an opportunity to create something new, meaningful, and even transcendent. Whether through art, writing, healing practices, or other forms of innovative expression, Radiant Alchemists have the unique ability to take the raw material of their trauma and turn it into something that not only heals themselves but also inspires and uplifts others.

The Core Qualities of the Radiant Alchemist

At the heart of the Radiant Alchemist is the power of transformation. While many people view trauma as something that breaks or diminishes them, the Radiant Alchemist embraces it as an opportunity to grow, evolve, and emerge stronger, becoming something even more extraordinary than before. They possess an innate ability to find light even in the darkest of times, using their creative energy to guide them through the healing process. This archetype embodies a profound resilience that allows them to adapt and transcend their pain, often becoming more compassionate, wise, and creative in the process.

The Radiant Alchemist thrives on creativity, and this is their defining characteristic. Whether through artistic expression, innovative problem-solving, or visionary thinking, the Radiant Alchemist channels their emotions into creative outlets that not only heal but also inspire. More than a coping mechanism, their creativity becomes a powerful tool for navigating their trauma and finding meaning in the chaos. They understand that creation is a form of healing, and through this process, they learn to reclaim their power and reframe the narrative of their trauma in a way that serves their personal evolution.

Resilience is another core quality of the Radiant Alchemist. Even when faced with overwhelming challenges or setbacks, they continue to rise, adapting and evolving in ways that allow them to transform adversity into opportunity. Their resilience is not just about survival—it's about thriving in the aftermath of trauma, using the experience to fuel their growth and their purpose. This strength allows them to see obstacles not as roadblocks, but turn them into stepping stones, and opportunities for growth and mastery, moving forward with grace and determination.

Empathy is another key trait of the Radiant Alchemist. Having experienced pain and transformation themselves, they develop a deep understanding and compassion for others who are also navigating difficult paths. Their ability to connect with others, often through their creative expressions, allows them to offer a unique form of support and encouragement. Their empathy helps them bridge the gap between their personal healing journey and the broader impact they can have on their community and the world.

The Challenges of the Radiant Alchemist

Despite their incredible potential for transformation, the Radiant Alchemist faces certain challenges on their journey to post-traumatic growth.

While they shine with the light of transformation, they must also navigate the shadows that accompany their journey. Their path is not without challenges, and the qualities that make them powerful can sometimes also become sources of struggle. A key aspect of the Radiant Alchemist's journey is learning to balance the light and dark within themselves.

One of the biggest obstacles they encounter is the temptation to bypass their pain in favour of immediate transformation. Because they are so attuned to the idea of turning their pain into purpose, they may be tempted to move too quickly, trying to avoid or numb their emotions rather than fully experiencing and processing them.

While their desire to find purpose and meaning is admirable, it's really important for Radiant Alchemists to honour their emotions, sit with the discomfort and allow themselves the space to heal, rather than rushing through the process, and therefore allowing the natural process of healing to unfold.

The Radiant Alchemist must remember that true transformation does not come from denying or bypassing pain—it comes from acknowledging it fully and using it as fuel for growth. Honouring their emotions, no matter how difficult, is essential for sustainable healing. When they can allow themselves to feel deeply, without rushing to fix or to transform, then they create the conditions for authentic and profound change.

Radiant Alchemists may also struggle with the burden of expectation. Because they are so adept at turning pain into purpose, they may feel pressure—either self-imposed or from others—to always be "radiant", positive, and productive even when they are still processing their own trauma.

Because they are often seen as beacons of inspiration, there may be an unspoken expectation that they must constantly be "on," always creating, always uplifting. This pressure can lead to emotional exhaustion and a sense of disconnection from their authentic true feelings. Radiant Alchemists need to remember that they are allowed to feel the full spectrum of emotions, not just the "positive" ones.

By giving themselves permission to be vulnerable and imperfect, they can then create space for deeper healing and prevent burnout. It's important for the Radiant Alchemist to embrace their humanness, whilst understanding that their light shines even brighter when they choose to honour their moments of darkness.

While creativity is the greatest strength of the Radiant Alchemist, it can also become a double-edged sword. They may sometimes become overly attached to their creative outlets and use these as a means of escape rather than for healing.

While creativity is a powerful tool for transformation, it's essential that Radiant Alchemists use it in a way that fosters healing rather than avoidance. They may use this over-attachment to creative pursuits to avoid confronting their deeper emotional wounds. They must learn to strike a balance between creativity, self-expression and self-care, ensuring that their creative pursuits are a tool for processing emotions, and in service of healing (rather than an avenue for avoidance) and truly serving their healing journey. By staying mindful of their motivations, the Radiant Alchemist can ensure that their creative pursuits are truly aligned with their healing journey.

Embracing Shadow Work and the Art of Alchemy

In order for the Radiant Alchemist to truly unlock their potential, they must be willing to engage in shadow work. This type of work involves confronting the aspects of themselves that they may be tempted to avoid or deny, such as anger, fear, shame, and grief. Shadow work is an essential part of the alchemical process, as it allows the Radiant Alchemist to transform the "base metals" of their emotional experience into "gold".

Shadow work is not easy, yet it is incredibly rewarding. By facing their darkest emotions, Radiant Alchemists gain a deeper understanding of themselves and their trauma. They learn to embrace the parts of themselves that they may have once rejected, and in doing so, they become whole. This process of integration is at the heart of their transformation—it is how they turn pain into purpose.

For many Radiant Alchemists, their artistic and creative expressions become the medium through which they do their shadow work. Through painting, writing, music, dance, and other forms of expression, they can confront and process their emotions in a way that feels safe and meaningful. This creative process becomes a form of therapy, allowing them to explore their shadow side and then transform it into something beautiful.

Amplifying the Creative and Transformative Powers of the Radiant Alchemist

The Radiant Alchemist has immense potential for transformation and one of the most powerful ways that they can enhance their journey toward post-traumatic growth is by consciously cultivating and amplifying their creative and transformative powers. By leaning into their natural gifts and incorporating practices that support their creativity and transformation, the Radiant Alchemist can accelerate their growth, deepen their healing process and step into their full potential.

Here are some practices and exercises that can help Radiant Alchemists harness their creative energy and amplify their creative and transformative abilities:

1. **Creative Expression as Healing:** One of the most effective and powerful tools available for the Radiant Alchemist is creative expression. Whether it's through painting, writing, dancing, music or any other form of artistic outlet, creativity allows them to channel their emotions into something tangible and transformative. By engaging in creative practices regularly, the Radiant Alchemist can deepen their healing and discover new insights about themselves.

   To amplify this powerful process, set aside dedicated time each week for creative practices, allowing yourself to explore different mediums without judgment. Focus on the process itself, allowing your emotions to flow freely through your chosen medium. Remember, the goal is not perfection or how others will perceive your work—it's a way to engage in self-expression and healing.

2. **Journalling for Transformation:** Journalling is a powerful practice that can help Radiant Alchemists gain clarity and insight into your emotions. Use the journal as a space to reflect on your experiences, and to process emotions. By putting your thoughts and feelings into words, you can begin to see patterns, uncover hidden truths, and explore how your pain can be transformed into purpose.

Consider using journalling prompts like this,

- "What can I create from this experience?" or
- "How can I use this challenge to fuel my growth?" or
- "What lesson is this pain teaching me?"

Journalling can also be used to track your progress and to reflect on how far you've come as it can be very easy to lose sight of how far along the path you have travelled when you're deeply immersed in the daily experiences of the journey. By documenting your journey, you create a written testament to your transformation—a reminder of your strength and resilience.

3. **Visualisation and Manifestation:** Radiant Alchemists have a natural gift for envisioning possibilities and manifesting their desired outcomes. Incorporate visualisation practices into your daily routine, as this can help you to stay focused on your goals and imagining

yourself not just surviving but thriving and transforming. Visualise your pain dissolving into light and fuelling your creative energy, propelling you toward your goals and dreams.

See yourself fully transformed, living with purpose and joy. By holding this vision in your mind, you can create a powerful energetic blueprint that guides your actions and supports your growth.

4. **Alchemy of Emotions Meditation:** Meditation can be a profound way for Radiant Alchemists to work with their emotions and transform them into something healing. One practice is the Alchemy of Emotions Meditation, where you create a meditation practice that focuses on visualising your emotions as raw materials, waiting to be transformed into something new. Sit quietly and focus on your emotions.

   Imagine them as different elements—perhaps your anger feels like fire, your sadness like water, or your fear like earth. As you breathe, visualise these elements being transmuted into something new. See your anger transforming into motivation, your sadness into compassion, and your fear into courage.

   Allow yourself to sit with these emotions and visualise them evolving into something that supports your growth. By engaging in this practice regularly, you can deepen your emotional awareness.

5. **Nature and Healing Rituals:** Nature can be a powerful source of healing and inspiration for the Radiant Alchemist. By spending time outdoors, connecting with the natural world and observing the cycles of transformation in nature such as growth, decay and renewal, they can find symbolic reminders of the transformative process. They can consider creating rituals around the changing seasons, using them as an opportunity to reflect on their own journey of transformation.

   Allow the beauty and resilience of nature to inspire your own healing process. For example, in the spring, you might focus on planting new seeds of intention, while in the autumn, you could reflect on letting go of old patterns or beliefs that no longer serve you. By aligning your healing process with the cycles of nature, you can tap into a deeper sense of connection and resilience.

6. **Service and Purpose:** Radiant Alchemists often find great meaning and fulfillment in helping others. By sharing their journey and offering support to those who are struggling, they not only amplify their own healing but also make a positive impact on the world. Consider how you can use your experience and transformation to serve others, whether through mentorship, volunteering, or creative projects that inspire and uplift those who are struggling. By focusing on service, the Radiant Alchemist reinforces the idea that their pain has purpose, and by sharing your journey and offering support, you can amplify your own healing while also making a positive impact in the lives of others.

Embracing Growth as a Radiant Alchemist

If you feel you could be a Radiant Alchemist, then the key to accelerating your path to post traumatic growth lies in using your extraordinary ability to turn your pain into purpose, through using your creativity to heal and inspire. By embracing your natural gifts and leaning into your creative powers, you can accelerate your growth and step into a life of meaning, fulfillment and radiance that is not just about surviving—but thriving.

It is important to remember though that your healing is a process, and it's okay to take your time. Don't feel pressured to rush through your emotions or bypass your pain in favour of immediate transformation. Instead, honour your journey and trust that your creative energy will guide you toward healing in the way that is right for you.

The path of the Radiant Alchemist is not always easy, but it is profoundly rewarding. As you continue on your journey, remember that your pain does not define you—it is simply the raw material from which you will create something extraordinary. Through your creativity, resilience, and empathy, you will not only heal yourself, but also become a beacon of hope for others who are walking the path of trauma and transformation.

The light you create is the light that will guide you forward. Embrace your power as a Radiant Alchemist and watch as your life transforms before your eyes.

Case Study: Liane's Transformation from Trauma to Alchemy

Liane's story embodies the essence of the Radiant Alchemist. After experiencing significant loss, Liane found herself consumed by grief and despair. But rather than allowing her pain to define her, she began to channel her emotions into creative outlets. She started journalling to process what had happened and found that by doing this, considerable emotions began to surface. This felt extremely uncomfortable however Liane knew she really needed to feel her emotions rather than bypass them, in order to feel better at a deeper level. So, she then used painting as a way to process her grief, and over time, her art became a powerful tool for healing. Each brushstroke allowed her to release her pain and transform it into something beautiful.

As Liane continued to explore her creativity, she found a deeper sense of purpose emerging. She realised that her art wasn't just helping her to feel better and improving her overall well-being, it was inspiring others who had been through similar experiences.

Liane began sharing her story and artwork with the world, and she discovered a profound sense of fulfillment. Her trauma had been the catalyst for her growth, and through her artwork, she had become a Radiant Alchemist—someone who could transform pain into purpose and light.

In the next chapter, we will explore another archetype with its own unique approach to healing. For now, continue to nurture your creative spirit, embrace your power to transform, and allow your light to shine as brightly as possible.

Conclusion: The Radiant Alchemist's Journey to Healing

The Radiant Alchemist embodies one of the most empowering and transformative paths in the process of post-traumatic growth. This archetype reminds us that while pain is inevitable, it can be alchemised into purpose, creativity, and healing. Through embracing their capacity for resilience, empathy, and creative expression, Radiant Alchemists turn their trauma into something profoundly beautiful—not only for themselves but for those around them.

To walk the path of the Radiant Alchemist is to understand that your trauma does not have to be a final chapter in your story. Instead, it can serve as the raw material for transformation, offering you the opportunity to create a life filled with meaning and radiance. As a Radiant Alchemist your power lies in your ability to use the experiences of the past to fuel your future, continually evolving and finding deeper purpose with each step forward.

As you explore this archetype, remember that your journey from pain to purpose is unique. Allow yourself to engage deeply in the process of self-reflection, creativity, and transformation. You are not defined by your trauma—you are the alchemist who has the power to transform it into something far greater.

The Radiant Alchemist invites you to embrace your potential for growth and transformation, trusting that even in the darkest moments, you hold the ability to create light. This light is your gift to yourself and the world, a testament to the strength and resilience that lives within you.

CHAPTER 10

The Liberated Voyager

-

Embracing Freedom

"Life is either a daring adventure or nothing at all."

— Helen Keller

The Liberated Voyager archetype represents the deep yearning for freedom, exploration, and self-discovery that often emerges after a period of profound trauma.

When someone embodies the Liberated Voyager, they are drawn toward new horizons, eager to embrace life with a sense of curiosity and courage. These Voyagers have an unrelenting desire to experience the world on their own terms, unburdened by the chains of past trauma. For them, instead of being defined by the past, they actively rewrite their story, and navigating life after adversity becomes a grand adventure, full of potential, growth, and new beginnings.

For many, trauma can feel like a prison—a place of restriction, isolation, and limitation. The Liberated Voyager breaks free from that confinement, seeking autonomy and new experiences, determined not to be defined by their past but to rewrite their story. They trust in their ability to navigate the unknown with grace, choosing to heal through exploration rather than avoidance. They see life as a continuous journey, and rather than shying away from change, they welcome it.

It is in the very act of exploration—whether external or internal—that the Liberated Voyager finds healing. They learn to trust themselves again, to seek new experiences, and to navigate the unknown with openness and grace, as they learn to balance the joy of adventure with the essential work of inner healing.

The Core Qualities of the Liberated Voyager

The Liberated Voyager's defining quality is their deep-rooted desire for freedom. After experiencing the restrictions that trauma can impose, Voyagers are determined to reclaim their independence and autonomy. They want to break free from any limitations - whether they be emotional, mental, or physical—that their trauma has placed upon them. Freedom becomes their guiding star, and they pursue it with unwavering determination.

For some Liberated Voyagers, freedom may manifest as physical travel, seeing them breaking away from their hometowns or familiar environments in search of new landscapes. For others, it could mean the freedom to express themselves creatively, spiritually, or intellectually. But at its core, freedom for the Liberated Voyager is an inner state, a release from the emotional shackles of the past.

As they heal, the Voyager learns that true liberation isn't just about breaking free from something; it's about stepping into the fullness of life. For them, it's about making choices that reflect their authentic self and living without the fear or restraint that once held them back.

Exploration is another key characteristic of the Liberated Voyager. This archetype is not content with staying in one place, whether that's a physical location, a mindset, or a way of being. They have a profound curiosity about the world and about themselves. Life is a series of discoveries, each one adding to their understanding of who they are and what they're capable of. Exploration can take many forms—it could be travelling to new places, trying new hobbies, deepening relationships, or even exploring different aspects of their personality and beliefs. For the Liberated Voyager, every experience holds the potential for growth and self-discovery.

Liberated Voyagers also tend to be drawn to the unfamiliar. They aren't content with comfort zones; they seek out the unknown and embrace the challenges that come with it. In so doing, they learn to trust themselves in new ways, building resilience and self-confidence with every new adventure.

Adaptability is a further strength that the Liberated Voyager possesses in abundance. Having survived trauma, they have learned to navigate life's uncertainties and are now equipped with the flexibility to face whatever comes their way. Rather than being feared, change is embraced as an opportunity for growth. The Liberated Voyager understands that life is not static; it's indeed a dynamic process of evolution. This adaptability allows them to move through life with a sense of ease and confidence, trusting that they can handle whatever challenges arise.

Even when the path ahead is unclear, the Liberated Voyager trusts their ability to navigate it. This ability to adapt is one of their greatest assets, making them resilient in the face of adversity.

The Challenges of the Liberated Voyager

Though the Liberated Voyager is driven by a thirst for freedom and exploration, they also face certain challenges along the way. Understanding these challenges is crucial for them in navigating the path to post-traumatic growth without losing balance.

One of the primary struggles for this archetype is the tendency to flee rather than face their emotions. In their quest for freedom, some Voyagers may develop an avoidance pattern, seeking external adventures to escape the internal discomfort of unresolved trauma.

While exploring the world and seeking new experiences can be empowering, it's essential for Voyagers to remember that true liberation involves not just external exploration of the world but also facing and integrating their emotions. If they focus too much on running from the past, they risk missing the opportunity for doing the deep healing they need.

Voyagers must be mindful of when they're using adventure as a distraction from the inner work that still needs to be done. It's essential for them to cultivate a sense of self-awareness, ensuring that their external journey is aligned with their internal one.

Another challenge for the Liberated Voyager is finding balance. They may be so eager to break free from their past that they neglect to establish a sense of stability. Constant movement and change, while exciting, can lead to exhaustion if not balanced with moments of stillness and reflection.

The Voyager must learn to strike a balance between their desire for freedom and the need for grounding. Just as a ship requires an anchor to stay secure amid turbulent waters, the Liberated Voyager needs practices that keep them centred and peaceful. They must learn that grounding themselves does not mean they are sacrificing their freedom. Rather, it provides the foundation they will need to continue their journey with strength and resilience.

Balancing movement with moments of stillness allows the Liberated Voyager to recharge, reflect, and to process their experiences. Without this balance, they risk burning out or becoming disconnected from their inner world.

Maintaining meaningful relationships can also be difficult for the Liberated Voyager, especially if they feel constrained by commitments or ties to others. While their independent spirit is one of their greatest strengths, it's also important for them to remember that connection and support from others are crucial components of healing.

They may fear that forming close bonds will compromise their freedom or tie them down in ways that feel restrictive. They may need to work on deepening their relationships without feeling as though their freedom is being compromised.

The journey of healing is often enriched by the presence of other supportive, empathetic people and the Voyager must find ways to balance their need for independence with their capacity for connection. True freedom does not require isolation; in fact, some of the most liberating experiences come from the relationships we cultivate.

Voyagers must work on creating relationships that honour their need for freedom while also fostering the connection and vulnerability they require. By cultivating a balance between independence and meaningful relationships, they can experience the joy of connection without feeling confined.

Embracing Freedom and Exploration as a Liberated Voyager

As a Liberated Voyager, your path to post-traumatic growth lies in the full embrace of freedom, exploration, and adventure.

Your willingness to step into the unknown and forge your own path is an incredible strength that will carry you far on your journey of healing. However, for growth to be sustainable, you must learn to integrate both the inner and outer aspects of your journey. True liberation is not only about external exploration but also about inner discovery.

To fully step into the Liberated Voyager archetype, it's essential that you balance your desire for adventure with moments of stillness and self-reflection. Here are some exercises that can help Liberated Voyagers embrace their journey while maintaining balance and peace:

1. **Mindful Exploration:** Set aside time to explore your surroundings mindfully. Whether it's going on a walk in nature, visiting a new place, or engaging in a new activity, aim to bring awareness to each experience. Notice how it feels to be fully present in the moment and allow yourself to engage with your environment. Mindful exploration will help you cultivate a deeper connection to your experiences and prevent you from using exploration as a means of escape.

2. **Grounding Practices:** To balance your adventurous spirit, it can help to incorporate grounding practices into your daily routine. This could include meditation, yoga, deep breathing exercises, or simply taking time each day to sit in stillness. These practices will help you stay centred and connected to yourself, even amid change. Grounding practices can serve as your anchor, helping you to maintain stability as you explore new horizons.

3. **Journalling for Self-Reflection:** Use journalling as a tool for inner exploration. After each new experience or adventure, take the time to reflect on what you've learned about yourself. Ask yourself questions like, "How has this experience changed me?" or "What emotions came up for me during this journey?" Journalling will help you to integrate your external experiences with your internal growth, leading to a deeper sense of self-awareness.

4. **Setting Intentions for Freedom:** Freedom is a core value for the Liberated Voyager, however, it's important to be intentional about what freedom means to you. Take your time to reflect on how you can create freedom in your life without avoiding your emotions or responsibilities. Set intentions that align with your values, and let these intentions guide your actions. Remember, true freedom comes from within—it's the ability to live authentically and to make choices that honour your soul's desires.

5. **Creating a Personal Sanctuary:** While the Liberated Voyager thrives on exploration, it's also important to have a place of refuge where you can rest and recharge. Create a personal sanctuary in your home—a space that feels peaceful, safe, and is nurturing. This can be a corner of a room, a meditation space, or even a cosy reading nook. It might even be a spot outside in your garden. Having a sanctuary will give you a place to retreat when you need to pause and reflect.

6. **Travel as a Metaphor for Healing:** For many Liberated Voyagers, travel and exploration are central to their identity. Use travel as a metaphor for your healing journey. Just as you would plan an adventure, approach your healing with curiosity and openness. Allow yourself to explore new perspectives, beliefs, and practices that support your growth. View each step of your healing as part of a greater adventure that is leading you toward wholeness.

7. **Embracing the Unknown:** The Liberated Voyager has a natural affinity for the unknown, but it can still be challenging to embrace uncertainty when it comes to your healing. Remind yourself that the unknown is often where growth happens. Practice surrendering to the uncertainty of your healing journey, trusting that each experience is guiding you toward greater freedom and fulfillment. Embrace change as a necessary part of your evolution.

8. **Building Meaningful Connections:** While independence is a strength of the Liberated Voyager, it's important not to isolate yourself from others. Make a concerted effort to build and maintain meaningful connections with people who respect your independence whilst also offering you support and understanding and who uplift you. These connections can provide a sense of belonging and offer valuable insights on your journey. Remember that you don't have to navigate your healing alone—allow others to accompany you on your voyage.

Embracing Growth as a Liberated Voyager

If you feel you could be a Liberated Voyager, accelerating your path to post traumatic growth comes through the interplay of exploration and self-reflection. It's undoubtedly in the act of stepping into the unknown—whether it's a new place, a new relationship, or a new mindset—that you will find healing. However, for growth to be sustainable, you must learn to integrate both the inner and outer aspects of your journey.

True freedom comes from within, and for you, inner exploration is just as important as external adventures. Healing requires going inward, facing your unresolved trauma, and allowing yourself to process any emotions fully. Practices such as meditation, journaling, and mindfulness can help you as the Liberated Voyager to reconnect with your inner world, making sure your external exploration aligns with your internal growth.

Action is a key element of your growth. By stepping into new experiences and making bold choices, you will embody the freedom you crave. Whether it's through travel, creative expression, or challenging yourself to try something new, these actions reinforce your belief that life can be lived on your own terms. Every step forward, no matter how small, is a victory over the trauma that once held you back.

As much as the Liberated Voyager thrives on movement, you must also embrace rest and reflection as essential parts of your journey. Taking time to process your experiences allows you to fully integrate what you've learned. Rest doesn't diminish your freedom; instead, it enhances your ability to sustain your journey over the long term. By alternating between action and reflection, the Liberated Voyager can grow in a balanced and holistic way.

Case Study: Molly's Journey Toward Freedom

Molly, a 36-year-old graphic designer, had always loved travelling. After enduring years of bullying and emotional trauma, as a child and young woman, she felt suffocated by her circumstances, yearning for freedom and independence. When she finally broke free from the toxic environment that had been holding her back, she embarked on a journey of self-discovery. She travelled to new places, tried new experiences, and began exploring parts of herself she had long ignored.

At first, Molly found solace in constant movement, using travel as a way to escape her painful memories. But over time, she realised that true freedom wasn't just about physical exploration—it was about emotional liberation and connection. She decided to settle down and enjoy a long-term relationship when she turned 30.

However, after the sudden loss of her partner in a tragic accident, at 35 years her world shrank. Molly found herself emotionally confined again, trapped in a cycle of grief and anxiety that made it difficult for her to engage with the life she had rebuilt and once loved. She became afraid of uncertainty, and the idea of travelling or even trying new things again seemed impossible.

After several months of therapy, Molly began to embrace the Liberated Voyager within her. She realised that, while her partner's death was a deep wound that had aggravated some of her pain from her younger days, it didn't have to define the rest of her life. She craved the freedom to explore again, not to run from her pain but to reconnect with the part of herself that thrived on adventure.

Molly started small—she took short trips to nearby towns, and over time, she expanded her travels further. Each new experience was a challenge, but it also brought healing. She began to journal during her trips, using her writing to process her grief and pain. By facing both her internal emotions and her external fears, Molly found that her travels became less about escape and more about rediscovery.

Through this process, Molly learned to balance her need for exploration with moments of stillness. She created a sanctuary at home—a quiet space where she could rest, reflect, and recharge between adventures. Molly also reconnected with friends who were safe and supportive, allowing herself to be vulnerable and share her journey with others. This balance of independence and connection helped her heal in a deeper way than she had ever imagined.

She began incorporating grounding practices into her routine and set intentions for how she wanted to create freedom in her life. Molly's healing journey became a delicate dance between adventure and stillness, and with each step, she grew stronger and more empowered.

Molly's story illustrates the power of the Liberated Voyager archetype—one that seeks freedom, not just externally but internally. By embracing both exploration and reflection, Molly found a sense of peace and purpose that had eluded her for so long. While her partner's loss will always be part of her story, it no longer defines her. Instead, she defines her life through her own choices—guided by curiosity, courage, and a deep sense of inner freedom.

Conclusion: Becoming the Liberated Voyager

As a Liberated Voyager your journey is one of continuous exploration of the world, or yourself, and of the possibilities that lie ahead for freedom and growth. Trauma may have confined you, but now you are free to reclaim your life on your terms.

As you step into this archetype, remember that true liberation involves both external adventures and inner healing. You are not defined by your trauma; rather, you can use it as a catalyst for growth and transformation. Your thirst for freedom and your curiosity about life will take you far but remember to balance your adventures with moments of stillness and self-reflection.

By balancing exploration with reflection, action with rest, and independence with connection, you will thrive on your journey toward post-traumatic growth.

The world is full of possibilities waiting to be explored, and as a Liberated Voyager, you have the strength, resilience, and curiosity to embrace them. Trust your inner compass and continue to seek out new horizons. Life after trauma is not about simply surviving—it's about living fully and discovering all that you are capable of becoming. By integrating the two forces of expansion and grounding you will find a deep sense of liberation and fulfillment.

CHAPTER 11

Identifying Your Archetypes
-
Keys to Post-Traumatic Growth

> "Knowing yourself is the beginning of all wisdom."
>
> —Aristotle

T he journey of healing and transformation is an intricate dance between self-awareness and taking purposeful action. One of the most empowering ways to cultivate that awareness is by identifying your primary archetype(s).

Your archetype represents the essence of who you are at your core. An archetype is not just a label. It is an expression of your core strengths, the challenges you face, the ways in which you respond to adversity and trauma, which in turn define how you move through these experiences. By recognising your archetype(s), you can unlock the door to post-traumatic growth (PTG), accelerating your journey from surviving to thriving.

It's important to remember that you are not limited to a single archetype. We are complex beings, shaped by multifaceted experiences, and often embody different archetypes at various points in our lives. Therefore, our healing too is multifaceted, and we will embody different archetypes at various points in our healing journey.

That's why, in this chapter, we will explore how to identify your top three archetypes, creating what I call your **Archetype Profile©**. This profile is a powerful tool for self-discovery and growth and becomes your personalised compass, guiding you as you navigate the dynamic process of healing and transformation.

We will dive deeply into the process of identifying your top three archetypes, providing reflective exercises and practical strategies to extend your understanding of yourself. We'll also explore how your archetypes can shift as you move through different phases of healing, giving you the flexibility and insight to embrace your evolution with grace.

First, let's take a step back and understand the importance of recognising and working with these archetypes as you move through the healing process.

The Power of Archetypes in the Healing Process

By its very nature, trauma distorts our sense of self. It fractures our confidence, leaves us feeling disconnected, and often creates confusion about who we are. It's not uncommon for trauma survivors to feel that their core identity has been lost or obscured by their experience.

One of the most challenging aspects of post-traumatic growth is reclaiming that identity and rebuilding a sense of self that is rooted not in the trauma, but in the strength, resilience, and wisdom gained from overcoming it.

This is where archetypes become such a powerful tool. Archetypes represent universal patterns of behaviour and energy that transcend time and culture. By identifying your archetypes, you can begin to understand the core strengths that have shaped your survival and healing journey, as well as the challenges that may still be standing in your way.

Why Identifying Your Archetype is Essential to Post-Traumatic Growth

Just as you wouldn't embark on a journey without a map, you shouldn't embark on your healing journey without a clear understanding of who you are, and also, how you tend to respond to challenges. Identifying your archetype profile is like having a personalised roadmap to guide you through the complex terrain of healing. It offers you clarity, direction, and a profound sense of empowerment.

When we experience trauma, it is easy to feel lost, unsure of ourselves, and uncertain about how to move forward. Trauma can shake our foundation, leaving us questioning our identity, our strengths, and our purpose. This was my personal experience when I went through considerable trauma some years ago (if you would like to know more, read my chapter in the *Empowered Women Empower Women* book).

My life felt fractured, my sense of self shattered, and it wasn't until I began to understand the ways that trauma had shaped my responses that I could find my way back to feeling whole. One of the most powerful tools in this journey was discovering my trauma archetypes.

Your archetypes provide a deep sense of validation—knowing that your struggles, behaviours, and patterns are not random, but are rooted in a specific archetypal energy that has developed as a response to your trauma experiences. This liberating awareness shifts the focus from "What's wrong with me?" to "How can I make sense of what has happened to me, embrace my strengths and use them to thrive?"

While each archetype provides a unique lens through which to view your healing journey, it's important to acknowledge the subtle but significant differences between them. Many archetypes may share similar qualities- such as resilience, creativity, or a desire for connection- yet the way these traits manifest and are harnessed differs from one archetype to the next. These distinctions are crucial in understanding how to approach each archetype's strengths and challenges. By recognising these nuances, you can tailor your growth strategies more effectively, ensuring you're working with the natural tendencies of your archetype to accelerate your transformation. This is what empowers you to not only heal but to thrive in alignment with who you truly are.

Consider the **Phoenix Riser**, for instance. This archetype thrives in times of destruction and chaos, finding the strength to rise from the ashes time and again. They may initially feel overwhelmed by the constant need to rebuild and rise from the ashes of their trauma, but when they realise that this archetype gives them strength, resilience, and adaptability, they can learn to leverage these qualities as powerful tools for growth.

By comparison, the **Resilient Sage** is grounded in wisdom and reflection, drawing strength from their ability to pause, evaluate, and extract valuable lessons from every experience, allowing them to navigate their journey with a sense of calm and purpose.

Both archetypes offer powerful insights into how a person might navigate trauma, yet they also come with their own unique challenges. The **Phoenix Riser** may struggle with burnout from constantly having to rebuild, while the **Resilient Sage** may feel paralysed by over-analysis. Similarly, a **Reflective Orchestrator** may struggle with overthinking or indecision, yet this archetype can also provide invaluable insight and deep emotional intelligence if harnessed appropriately.

Identifying your archetypes allows you to work *with* your unique strengths and challenges, rather than *against* them. It helps you to tailor your healing journey in a way that feels authentic, aligned, and sustainable for you. You are no longer trying to fit yourself into a 'one-size-fits-all' model of healing; instead, you are creating a path that is uniquely yours to navigate.

Understanding these dynamics is crucial for moving forward. Your archetype profile provides a framework for recognising not only the strengths you bring to your healing journey but also the potential pitfalls you could face. It gives you the self-awareness needed to overcome those challenges, enabling you to consciously cultivate your growth.

The Intersection of Multiple Archetypes

While one archetype may dominate your personality, it's likely that you embody several. Healing is rarely linear, and as you progress through different stages of your recovery, you may shift between archetypes. This is why creating an *Archetype Profile* is so important, as it allows for fluidity and growth.

Let's take a moment to explore what this might look like in practice. Imagine you are primarily a **Reflective Orchestrator**— you are thoughtful, meticulous, and highly introspective. You are someone who likes to take your time, analyse every angle, and carefully weigh up your decisions. While this is a strength in many ways, it can also lead to periods of stagnation for you, where overthinking keeps you from taking any action.

However, during a particularly challenging time, you may find yourself tapping into the **Phoenix Riser** archetype, rising from the ashes of your own analysis paralysis with newfound energy and determination. In this way, your healing process may oscillate between reflection and action, thoughtfulness and resilience.

This interplay between archetypes is natural, and it's important to embrace it rather than trying to force yourself into a rigid and ultimately narrow definition of who you are. Allowing for this kind of fluidity in your healing journey makes the process not only more effective and powerful, but also more compassionate overall. It gives you permission to be human, to shift and change as needed, and to embrace the full complexity of who you are.

Deepening Self-Understanding: Exercises to Help You Identify Your Primary Archetypes

Identifying your archetypes requires a deep level of introspection and self-reflection. It's not something that happens overnight, rather a gradual process of discovery. To begin identifying your primary archetype(s), approach the process with curiosity, self-compassion, and openness. Below are several exercises designed to help you begin this journey. Take your time with each one, allowing yourself to explore your thoughts and feelings fully.

1. **Reflect on Your Trauma Journey and Past Experiences of Growth**

    One of the best ways to begin identifying your primary archetypes is by taking a moment to reflect on your past trauma experiences or where you've overcome adversity. Consider the ways in which you have responded to adversity, both in the past and in the present. What strengths have emerged from your experiences? What challenges or patterns have you noticed?

    Often, the archetypes that emerge during these times are the ones most dominant in your personality.

    Journal Prompts:

    - Think back to a time when you faced a major life challenge. How did you respond?
    - What strengths did you draw upon to get through it?

- What personal qualities have helped you navigate difficult situations?
- How do you typically approach challenges—head-on with action, or do you take a more reflective, cautious approach?
- What is your greatest challenge when it comes to healing?
- What do you admire most about how you have handled past adversity?

As you reflect on these questions and start writing down your thoughts, you may begin to see patterns emerge. Perhaps you've always been a **Phoenix Riser**, using resilience and determination to rebuild after your setbacks. Or maybe you see yourself more in the **Authentic Warrior**, as someone who faces challenges with raw honesty and emotional strength.

2. Take the Trauma Archetypes Quiz©

To further hone-in on your specific archetypes, consider taking the Trauma Archetypes Quiz©. This quiz will guide you through your responses to trauma, coping strategies and unique strengths, providing an Archetype Profile© that reflects who you are in the context of your healing journey.

To complete the quiz go to **https://drnataliegreen.com.au/trauma-archetypes-quiz/**

Reflect on Your Results: Once you've completed the quiz, take some time to sit with the results. Reflect on how your top three archetypes resonate with you and how they currently show up in your life. Ask yourself:

- Do these archetypes feel aligned with my experiences and strengths?
- How do these archetypes inform the way I approach healing and growth?

3. **Explore Your Top Three Archetypes**

   After identifying your top three archetypes, explore each one in depth. Review the qualities, strengths, and challenges of each archetype, and then reflect on how these aspects tend to show up in your life.

   For example:

   - If you identify as a **Phoenix Riser**, reflect on how resilience and adaptability have helped you rebuild your life after trauma. Consider how you can continue to use these strengths to grow even more.
   - If you identify as a **Resilient Sage**, think about how wisdom and reflection have guided your healing thus far. How can you continue to tap into your inner wisdom to support your journey even more?
   - If you identify as a **Radiant Alchemist**, consider how your ability to transform your pain into purpose has shaped your experiences. How can you further harness your creative energy for continued growth?

4. **Identify Your Core Values**

   Your archetypes are deeply connected to your core values—the things that matter most to you and that tend to guide your decisions in life. By identifying your values, you can gain deeper insight into the archetypal energy that drives you.

Journal Prompts:

- What are the top five values that guide your life? (Examples might include resilience, authenticity, compassion, wisdom, or independence.)
- How have these values influenced your healing journey so far?
- In what ways do you think your values shape how you interact with others and the world around you?

For example, if independence is one of your core values, you might resonate with the **Liberated Voyager**, who seeks freedom and adventure as part of their healing journey. If wisdom and reflection are central to your life, you may identify more with the **Resilient Sage**, whose healing is rooted in deep introspection.

5. Notice Your Responses to Trauma Triggers

Trauma triggers can evoke strong emotional reactions, and the way we respond to these triggers can provide valuable clues about our archetypes. Do you tend to withdraw and reflect when triggered, or do you fight back with action and determination? Do you seek connection and support, or do you prefer to go it alone?

Journal Prompts:

- How do I typically respond when I'm feeling triggered or overwhelmed by trauma memories and experiences?
- What coping mechanisms have I developed to navigate these moments?
- How do these responses reflect my core strengths and my values?

For instance, a **Radiant Alchemist** may respond to trauma triggers by transforming their pain into creative expression—whether through art, writing, or some other form of creative outlet. Whilst, the **Empowered Trailblazer**, on the other hand, may respond with action, channelling their energy into advocacy or leadership roles that help others overcome similar challenges.

Reclaiming Your True Identity

One of the most transformative aspects of post-traumatic growth is reconnecting with your identity. As we know, trauma often has a way of distorting how we tend to see ourselves, leaving us feeling lost, fragmented, full of self-doubt or even disconnected from who we once were. As you heal, it's essential to not only rediscover who you are but also to honour the ways in which trauma has reshaped your sense of self.

Your identity is more than just the sum of your experiences- it's the essence of who you are, including your values (which we have already looked at), your beliefs, strengths, and aspirations.

Trauma can shift this in profound ways, but within that shift lies a real opportunity for growth. Rather than viewing your identity as something that's been "broken", you can reframe it as something that's evolving. Just as trauma changes you, healing can change you too - leading you to a deeper, and more authentic understanding of yourself.

The Role of Trauma in Shaping Identity

After experiencing trauma, it's very common to feel a sense of loss about who you were before. You may feel as if parts of your identity have been stripped away, or that you've had to "become someone else" just to survive. This survival mode, while necessary in the moment, can create a version of yourself that feels disconnected from your core.

However, your identity after trauma is not simply a reaction to what happened to you. It's an opportunity to reclaim your sense of self and decide who you want to be. This isn't about returning to the "old you", as you can't change what has happened, but rather about discovering a new, and more resilient version of yourself - one who now embodies strength, wisdom, and the capacity to thrive.

Exercises to Reconnect with Your True Identity

1. **Reflect on Who You Were Before Your Trauma** Begin by reflecting on who you were before the trauma occurred. What were your passions, interests, and dreams? What qualities did you admire in yourself, and how did you define your identity at that time?

   Write down:
   - What activities brought me joy before my trauma?
   - How did I view myself in terms of strengths and weaknesses?
   - What were my core beliefs and values?

2. **Recognise the Parts of Your Identity You've Retained** Even though trauma may have altered some aspects of your identity, there are likely still core parts of yourself that have remained constant. These could be your sense of humour, your love for certain activities, or your ability to connect with others.

   Reflect on:
   - What qualities have remained consistent, despite everything I've been through?
   - In what ways have I stayed true to myself?

3. **Explore the New Parts of Your Identity** Trauma doesn't just take away - it also has the potential to add new dimensions to your identity. You may have developed new strengths, such as resilience, empathy, or a deeper understanding of life's complexities. Embracing these aspects can help you feel more whole and authentic.

Consider:
- What new strengths or qualities have emerged because of my trauma?
- How has my worldview shifted?
- What aspects of myself have grown or transformed?

4. **Identify the Identity Shifts You Want to Keep** Not all changes in identity are negative. Some shifts may align more closely with who you truly are. For instance, trauma might have led you to be more introspective or compassionate. You may have developed a stronger sense of purpose or a clearer idea of what really matters most to you. These changes can be gifts - ways that your identity has evolved to better reflect your core self.

Ask yourself:
- What parts of my post-trauma identity feel authentic to who I truly am?
- How can I honour these new parts of myself even more?

5. **Visualise Your Future Self** Spend time envisioning the person you want to become. This isn't about striving for perfection or going back to the "old you" but instead about integrating the lessons of your trauma and your learnings into your identity. What does your "healed self" look like? How do you show up in the world?

Visualise:
- What does my most authentic self, look like in the future?
- How do I express my values, beliefs, and strengths?

- What kind of relationships do I want to have, and what kind of life do I want to lead?

By recognising that trauma has undoubtedly reshaped (but not destroyed) your identity, you can reclaim your sense of self with purpose. This process is about choosing who you really want to be, rather than letting trauma define you. It's an opportunity to step into a more authentic version of yourself - one who embraces both the light and the dark and moves forward with clarity, courage, and resilience.

The Intersection of Core Values and Identity

Your identity and your core values are deeply intertwined. When you get clear on your values, you gain a more profound understanding of who you are at your core. Similarly, as you redefine your identity after trauma, you'll find that your core values often guide the way and serve as your compass.

Together, these elements form a strong foundation for post-traumatic growth, empowering you to move forward with greater self-awareness and authenticity. As you continue your healing journey, your archetype profile will serve as a powerful tool to help you integrate with your core values and reclaim and establish your identity - allowing you to step fully into your strength, wisdom, and potential.

Archetype Case Studies: Real-Life Applications

Sometimes, it can be helpful to see how the archetypes play out in real life. Below are some case studies of people who have successfully identified their archetypes and used this understanding to facilitate and accelerate their post-traumatic growth.

Case Study 1: Sally – The Phoenix Riser and Authentic Warrior

Sally, a 42-year-old trauma survivor, had always been someone who embodied resilience. After losing her partner in an accident, she found herself at rock bottom, grappling with profound grief and uncertainty. Yet, through sheer determination, Sally began to rebuild her life, finding new meaning and purpose along the way. As she reflected on her journey, it became clear that she embodied the **Phoenix Riser** archetype—someone who rises from the ashes of destruction time and again, stronger and wiser than before.

However, Sally's story didn't end there. As she delved deeper into her healing process, she also recognised the presence of the **Authentic Warrior** archetype. Sally had always been someone who wore her heart on her sleeve, facing her emotions head-on with raw honesty. This authenticity became a powerful tool in her healing, allowing her to connect with others who had experienced similar losses, and ultimately retrain as a grief counsellor.

Identifying both the **Phoenix Riser** and **Authentic Warrior** archetypes was key to Sally's post-traumatic growth. She learned to honour her strength while also embracing her vulnerability, creating a healing journey that was both empowering and authentic.

Case Study 2: Michael – The Resilient Sage and Reflective Orchestrator

Michael, a 45-year-old therapist, had always prided himself on his ability to see the bigger picture. After experiencing burnout early in his career, he took a step back and reflected on what had led him to that point. Through deep introspection, Michael recognised that he embodied the **Resilient Sage** archetype— someone who navigates life with wisdom, reflection, and emotional intelligence.

Michael also noticed that his over-reliance on reflection had, at times, led to indecision and stagnation. He realised that he had been operating as a **Reflective Orchestrator** - meticulously planning every step of his healing journey but often hesitating to act, which had led to him becoming quite stuck. This insight helped Michael find a balance between reflection and action, allowing him to move forward with greater confidence and clarity.

By identifying these two archetypes, Michael was able to better draw on his strengths to create a more balanced approach to his healing and professional growth. He learned to trust his analytical mind and his intuitive heart, using both as powerful tools to work sustainably for himself and in his work with clients.

Conclusion: Embracing Your Archetypes for Lasting Transformation

Identifying your archetypes is just the beginning. As you progress through your healing journey, your *Archetype Profile©* becomes a living, breathing guide - a dynamic map that helps you navigate the complexities of post-traumatic growth with greater awareness, clarity of purpose, and deeper compassion.

By understanding your archetypes, leaning into your strengths, working through your challenges, and staying open to change, you can accelerate your growth and create lasting, transformative change. Most importantly, you can begin to see yourself not as someone defined by trauma, but as someone empowered by the unique qualities that make you who you are.

Remember, healing is not a destination - it's a journey and it's constantly evolving. By identifying your archetypes, you've taken a powerful step toward reclaiming your true self and creating a life that is rooted in strength, resilience, and purpose.

CHAPTER 12

Harnessing Archetypes - Building Lasting Growth

"Post-traumatic growth is not just about bouncing back – it's about bouncing forward."

- Martin Seligman

Now that you've identified your archetypes and created your Archetype Profile©, the next step is to turn that knowledge into action. Understanding your archetypes is extremely powerful, however, it's only the first step in moving forward. What matters most is how you use this knowledge to create meaningful, lasting change in your life.

Archetypes are so much more than labels; they are dynamic, guiding forces that can help you to navigate the complexities of healing, developing resilience, and post-traumatic growth. They offer insight into your strengths, reveal your likely and potential challenges, and provide a roadmap for healing and personal transformation.

In this chapter, we'll take a deep dive into practical tips and strategies for harnessing the strengths of your archetypes while overcoming any associated challenges and learn some actionable strategies to harness the power of your archetypes in order to heal, grow and to thrive. By embracing your archetypes' unique qualities, you can turn your healing journey into one of growth and purpose.

In my personal journey of overcoming trauma, the various archetypes I tapped into along the way have helped me to reclaim my identity, build a future of resilience and get great clarity around my purpose. I know this is possible for others and I want this for you too.

The trauma I experienced could easily have left me stuck in survival mode and barely treading water. Instead, I was able to explore and identify the archetypes and access the unique strengths of my natural primary archetypes like the Phoenix Riser and Empowered Trailblazer, and then draw on my less comfortable ones such as the Reflective Orchestrator and the Radiant Alchemist. This didn't happen overnight—it was a process of transformation, requiring patience (which is generally not an area of strength for me), considerable self-reflection, and ultimately, the courage to evolve beyond my pain.

Whether you identify with the fierce independence of the Authentic Warrior, the wisdom of the Resilient Sage, or the transformational power of the Radiant Alchemist, you'll learn how to use your archetypes for daily empowerment and long-term growth.

Strategies for Each Archetype

As you know each archetype comes with its own set of strengths, challenges, and opportunities for growth. We will now break down those core qualities of each archetype and provide actionable strategies to help you leverage your strengths and overcome any potential obstacles, and use them as guiding forces for lasting growth.

The Phoenix Riser: Harnessing Resilience and Rebirth

As a Phoenix Riser, you have the innate ability to rise from the ashes. No matter how many times life knocks you down, your greatest strength is your capacity to rebuild after experiencing hardship. Your resilience is your superpower. This is an incredible gift and you've likely learned to adapt to life's changes with remarkable grace.

Strategies for the Phoenix Riser:

- **Embrace Your Strength**: Acknowledge your resilience and celebrate your ability to rebuild. Reflect on past experiences where you overcame adversity and use those memories a reminder of your power to rise again, and as fuel for future challenges.

- **Focus on Rebirth**: Rather than fearing change and viewing setbacks as failures, see them as opportunities for rebirth. Each challenge becomes a stepping stone to a stronger version of yourself. Visualise each setback as a step toward a new version of your that is stronger and wiser.

- **Set Boundaries**: The Phoenix Riser archetype can lead to burnout if you push yourself too hard. To avoid burnout, set and establish clear healthy boundaries that protect your energy. Remember, rising doesn't have to mean pushing yourself beyond your limits.

- **Create Rituals of Renewal**: Develop and incorporate daily or weekly rituals to support your rebirth and renewal. This could be daily affirmations, meditation, or engaging in self-care practices that recharge you and that help you stay grounded as you rebuild.

Personal Insight: As a Phoenix Riser, I faced burnout (often multiple bouts on an ongoing basis) from constantly rebuilding after traumatic experiences. By setting boundaries around my energy and creating rituals of renewal, especially enjoying a coffee by the beach at my favourite café, I have learned to pace myself and avoid exhaustion and turn each challenge into an opportunity for transformation.

The Resilient Sage: Leveraging Wisdom and Insight

Resilient Sages are known for being wise beyond their years. This wisdom is often developed through hard-earned life lessons, the deep insight gathered from life's challenges. You are adept at extracting meaning from difficult experiences and you have an incredible ability to see beyond the pain, using your experiences to guide yourself and others through similar challenges, towards healing.

Strategies for the Resilient Sage:

- **Trust Your Wisdom**: Lean into the deep wisdom you've cultivated through your experiences. Trust your intuition and the insights that arise from your inner knowing as you navigate your own healing journey.

- **Share Your Knowledge**: Use your insights to guide others, whether through writing, mentoring, or simply listening and being a supportive friend. Share the lessons you've learned to help others navigate their own healing journeys.

- **Practice Regular Reflection**: Make reflection a regular part of your daily or weekly practice. Journalling, meditation, or quiet contemplation can help you process new experiences and insights and deepen your self-awareness.

- **Balance Reflection with Action**: While introspection is your strength, Sages sometimes get stuck in reflection. Make sure to pair your introspection with purposeful action toward your goals and healing.

Personal Insight: This one was somewhat of a stretch for me as it did not come naturally. However, when I added in those times of reflection rather than constantly doing and rebuilding, I learnt to take on the strengths and some behaviours of a Resilient Sage. I found that reflection allowed me to understand my trauma on a deeper level. Yet there were moments when I got stuck in analysis, delaying action. Through ongoing practice, I discovered that by balancing reflection with purposeful steps, I found a healthier path to growth.

The Empowered Trailblazer: Leading with Courage and Innovation

Empowered Trailblazers are natural leaders, often carving and creating new pathways and breaking barriers in their healing journey. You have a pioneering spirit and are unafraid to break barriers or venture into uncharted territories of growth. As such, you have the courage to step into the unknown and lead others toward growth and transformation.

Strategies for the Empowered Trailblazer:

- **Take Bold Action:** Empowered Trailblazers thrive on action. Don't hesitate to take bold, decisive action towards your healing goals. Use your leadership skills to create the life you envision.

- **Balance Action with Self-Care:** While Trailblazers are action-oriented, it's really important to balance your drive with self-care to ensure that your drive to move forward doesn't lead to burnout. Build regular self-care into your routine. Take time to recharge so you can continue leading with strength.

- **Inspire Others:** Use your trailblazing spirit to inspire others. Your courage is contagious. Share your journey to inspire others to step into their own healing, whether through community work or sharing your story, your courage can motivate others to embark on their own healing journeys.

- **Be Open to New Paths**: Trailblazers can often feel pressured to keep forging ahead. Remember, that it's okay to pause, reflect, reassess, and adjust your course and change direction if needed.

Personal Insight: In my role as a Trailblazer, I have often pushed forward without stopping to rest. By understanding my strengths and fully exploring my challenge areas, I have learnt that pausing to recharge didn't make me weak. In fact, after one too many burnout episodes, I finally gave myself permission to completely cease work because that's what I needed to properly heal. This has taught me to read my body and recharge when needed. It has most definitely served to make me stronger, allowing me to continue leading with more clarity and purpose and to develop the post traumatic growth archetypes and bring this concept to life.

The Reflective Orchestrator: Tapping into Strategy and Patience

Reflective Orchestrators are strategic and patient and excel at seeing the bigger picture and creating thoughtful strategies. You are a natural planner and can plan your healing journey with care and thoughtfulness. You are patient in your approach, and deliberate in your healing journey, ensuring that each step you take is intentional and aligned with your values.

Strategies for the Reflective Orchestrator:

- **Create a Healing Plan:** Use your strategic thinking to map out your healing journey and create a clear plan. Set goals, create timelines and break down your goals into manageable steps.

- **Practice Patience:** Trust that your deliberate approach will lead to meaningful, long-term growth. Don't rush the process. Orchestrators understand that healing is a process, not a race. Practice patience and remind yourself that progress takes time.

- **Find Balance:** While planning is important, avoid overthinking or getting stuck in analysis paralysis. Balance your thoughtful approach with action.

- **Balance Strategy with Flexibility:** While planning is your strength, life can be unpredictable so allow space for flexibility and adaptability in your healing process.

- **Engage in Reflective Practices:** Incorporate regular reflection into your routine, such as journalling, meditating, or simply taking time to pause and reassess your progress.

- **Delegate When Needed:** Reflective Orchestrators sometimes take on too much. So, if you find yourself overwhelmed, don't hesitate to seek support from trusted allies.

Personal Insight: This archetype was my greatest stretch and the one that felt least natural for me. As I stepped into the Reflective Orchestrator archetype, I knew that creating a clear plan would help me feel more in control of my healing journey. However, I tend to prefer not to plan things out, as I have learnt from experience that plans tend to 'come undone'. So, I had to map out some goals, stay focused on following my path, whilst balancing the need to allow for flexibility and trust the process even when it didn't unfold exactly as expected.

The Authentic Warrior: Combining Strength with Vulnerability

Authentic Warriors are known for their fierce courage and deep authenticity. They are fiercely true to themselves, driven by a deep sense of integrity and inner strength. You fight for what you believe in, and your healing journey is centred around authenticity and standing in your truth. You lead with strength and aren't afraid to show your vulnerable side, making you a powerful force in the healing journey.

Strategies for the Authentic Warrior:

- **Show Up Fully and Stand in Your Truth**: Be unapologetically yourself, even in moments of vulnerability. Authenticity is your superpower. Stay true to who you are, even when it's difficult. Practice asserting your boundaries and speaking up for what you believe in.

- **Balance Strength with Softness:** While strength is a defining feature of the Authentic Warrior, remember that softness and vulnerability are equally powerful.

- **Embrace Your Strength and Vulnerability:** While Warriors are known for their strength, true courage comes from embracing vulnerability. Allow yourself to soften and be open to the support of others. Recognise the strength it takes to be vulnerable and open in your healing journey.

- **Set Boundaries and Prioritise Self-Care:** Warriors are often focused on others. While you're naturally open and authentic, it's important to protect your energy by setting clear boundaries with others. Make sure to prioritise self-care and nurture yourself along the way.

- **Celebrate Small Wins:** Acknowledge and celebrate every victory, no matter how small. Each step forward is a testament to your strength and resilience.

Personal Insight: The Authentic Warrior was overall a more natural archetype for me because I have always prided myself on my strength, however it hasn't always been this way. In the past I struggled to show vulnerability as I had been taught to 'be strong' and in my profession that was always reinforced. However, as I explored the archetypes concepts and was further along in my healing journey post-trauma, I recognised that once I embraced both my strengths and vulnerabilities, I became a more authentic and empowered version of myself.

The Radiant Alchemist: Transforming Pain into Purpose

Radiant Alchemists have a gift for transforming difficult experiences into something meaningful. You see potential in everything - even in the darkest of times - and use this potential to create beauty and purpose. You can take life's challenges and turn them into opportunities for growth, through creativity. Your ability to find light in the darkness is a testament to your resilience and creative power.

Strategies for the Radiant Alchemist:

- **Embrace Creative Expression**: Use your creative gifts as a means of processing trauma and finding healing. Whether through art, writing, music, or another medium, allow your creativity to be a channel for transformation and morph your pain into something beautiful and purposeful.

- **Find Purpose in Your Pain**: Seek to understand the lessons within your pain and use them as fuel for your personal growth.

- **Embrace Change**: As an Alchemist, you thrive on transformation. Embrace change as an essential part of your healing journey, trusting that it will lead to new opportunities for growth.

- **Balance Light and Shadow**: Alchemists tend to focus on finding the light in dark situations, but it's important to honour the shadow aspects of your experience too. Give yourself permission to grieve or feel pain without rushing to transform it.

- **Create Space for Creation**: Make time for regular creative practices that allow you to process your emotions and tap into your transformative power.

- **Practice Gratitude:** Gratitude is a powerful tool for helping with transformation. Regularly reflect on the things you are grateful for, even amid great hardship.

- **Cultivate Resilience:** While Alchemists are naturally resilient, it's important to nurture that resilience through self-care, support systems, and practices that ground you.

Personal Insight: I wasn't able to relate so naturally to the archetype as a Radiant Alchemist, either. However, as I moved through my trauma journey and into post-traumatic growth, I discovered that creativity was my way of making sense of the chaos in my life, and that through this I could tap into the most profoundly healing ways. By turning my pain into art and expression, I found purpose in my trauma through my writing and have grown beyond it and into post traumatic growth.

The Liberated Voyager: Exploring Freedom and Possibility

Liberated Voyagers thrive on freedom and are explorers at heart, always seeking new horizons and opportunities for growth. You thrive on exploration, adventure, and the endless possibilities that life offers. You are not content to stay stuck in the past—you are always seeking to move forward, grow, and experience the world in new ways.

Strategies for the Liberated Voyager:

- **Seek New Experiences**: Challenge yourself to step outside your comfort zone and explore new paths in your healing journey. Actively seek out new experiences that broaden your perspective and bring joy into your life. Travel, explore hobbies, or engage in activities that challenge and excite you.

- **Embrace Change**: Voyagers are natural adventurers and very adaptable and thrive in changing environments. Use this adaptability to navigate the ups and downs of healing. Embrace change as part of your journey. See each new chapter of your life as an opportunity for growth and exploration.

- **Balance Exploration with Grounding**: While exploration is key for Liberated Voyagers, balance it with stability as it's important to stay grounded as well. Develop grounding practices and routines to help you stay centred amidst change.

- **Practice Mindfulness:** Voyagers can sometimes get caught up in the thrill of the future. Practice mindfulness to stay present and appreciate the beauty of each moment.

- **Trust the Journey:** Trust that your path may not always be linear, but it will lead you exactly where you need to go.

Personal Insight: As I moved deeper through into post traumatic growth, I was able to more naturally tap into the Liberated Voyager archetype. I found freedom in letting go of the rigid expectations I had of myself and embracing the adventure of life. This allowed me to explore new possibilities for healing and growth, even in the face of uncertainty.

Working with Your Archetype Profile: Actionable Steps for Growth

Once you've created your Archetype Profile and gained insight into the archetypes that resonate with your trauma journey, the next step is to apply that understanding to your everyday life. Below are several strategies to help you work with your archetypes and foster post-traumatic growth.

1. Lean Into Your Strengths

Each archetype embodies unique strengths that you can harness to accelerate your healing journey. For instance, if you resonate most with the Liberated Voyager, you likely thrive on exploration, freedom, and new experiences. These strengths can become the foundation of your growth.

Exercise:

- List the key strengths associated with each of your archetypes.

- For each strength, brainstorm one practical way to integrate it into your healing journey. For example, a Liberated Voyager might challenge themselves to engage in a new hobby, or a Radiant Alchemist could focus on creative expression to process their emotions.

Personal Insight: When I realised I identified deeply with the Phoenix Riser and less so with the Radiant Alchemist, I leaned into their strengths and looked where the opportunities for growth were by constantly reimagining my life and embracing each challenge as an opportunity for rebirth. Creativity became my outlet, the channel allowing me to transform my pain into something meaningful.

2. Acknowledge and Work Through Your Challenges

Just as each archetype has its strengths, it also has its challenges. The Phoenix Riser, for example, may struggle with exhaustion from constantly having to rebuild. The Reflective Orchestrator might become paralysed by over-analysis. Recognising these challenges allows you to face them head-on.

Exercise:

- For each archetype in your profile, identify one challenge that might be holding you back.
- Brainstorm two ways you can work through this challenge. For instance, a Reflective Orchestrator might schedule regular check-ins with a mentor to avoid getting lost in analysis paralysis.

Personal Insight: As I said for me, initially, the Authentic Warrior archetype represented a challenge. It felt natural in many ways as I prided myself on my strength, but over time I realised that constantly fighting was keeping me from being vulnerable and therefore fully heal. Once I allowed myself to lean into vulnerability, I could integrate my strength with softness.

3. Create Rituals for Growth

Rituals serve as powerful anchors for grounding your healing journey in intentionality. By creating daily or weekly rituals that reflect your archetypes, you reinforce your strengths and become more equipped to face the inevitable challenges.

Exercise:

- Design a simple ritual that aligns with your archetypes. A Radiant Alchemist might set up a daily creative practice, like journalling or painting, while a Phoenix Riser could create rituals of renewal, like meditative reflection after stressful situations.

Personal Insight: One of the rituals I adopted as a Phoenix Riser was to start every morning with a meditation focused on renewal and regeneration. It helped me view each day as a new beginning, offering me space to rebuild, no matter how difficult the previous day had been.

4. Stay Open to Change

As has been mentioned, your archetype profile is not static, indeed it is dynamic as is your healing journey. As you grow, heal, and evolve, certain archetypes may rise in prominence while others fade into the background. This is natural and part of your personal evolution.

Exercise:

- Every few months, reflect on your healing journey and see if new archetypes have emerged or if others have become less dominant.
- Journal about how these shifts affect your personal growth. Are there new strengths that you can tap into, and opportunities for growth that you can now embrace?

Personal Insight: Initially, I identified strongly with the Authentic Warrior and Phoenix Riser archetypes, but over time, I began to embody the Liberated Voyager. As I moved further along the path beyond my trauma, the desire for freedom, exploration, and new horizons became central to my healing journey.

Embracing Your Unique Journey of Growth

No matter which archetypes you identify with, the key to lasting growth lies in embracing your unique journey. There is no one-size-fits-all approach to healing and that's indeed what's so exciting about these archetypes. Your path will be as unique as you are, shaped by your experiences, strengths, and the wisdom of your archetypes.

It's important to remember that growth is not linear. There will be moments of progress and moments of setback, and that's okay. What matters most is that you continue to move forward with intention, compassion, and a deep trust in your own resilience.

Each day, take time to connect with your archetypes. Use the strategies outlined in this chapter to harness your strengths, to look at how to overcome challenges, and to empower yourself to live a life of purpose, joy, and freedom.

You have everything you need within you to heal, grow, and to thrive. Trust in your journey, honour your progress, and know that the best is yet to come.

Conclusion: Stepping Fully into Your Power

Your archetypes are powerful tools for healing and growth, but they are just that—tools. The true power lies within you. By gaining a deep understanding of your archetypes and working with them intentionally, you can accelerate your post-traumatic growth journey and step fully into your power. Remember, healing is a process, and it's okay to take it one step at a time. You've already come so far – and now it's time to step into the next phase of your transformation with confidence, courage, and clarity.

CHAPTER 13

Combining Archetypes
-
Holistic Healing

"The whole is greater than the sum of its parts."

—Aristotle

As we move through life, we are rarely defined by just one identity, one role, or one way of being. The same applies to the Trauma Archetypes. While you may find yourself resonating deeply with one particular archetype, the beauty of healing in a holistic way lies in recognising that you are a complex, multifaceted being capable of drawing from the strengths of many of the archetypes. Healing, like life itself, is not linear but an intricate dance of energy, adaptation, and transformation.

In this chapter, we will explore how combining different archetypal energies can foster a more comprehensive, resilient, and empowered approach to our overall healing. By integrating multiple archetypes, you can create a powerful blend of inner resources to navigate your personal journey across all areas, whether it be in work, relationships, and/or personal growth.

The Interplay Between Archetypes: Harnessing Collective Strengths

One of the most transformative aspects of the Post-Traumatic Growth Archetypes is their ability to work together, enhancing one another's strengths and compensating for challenges and potential weaknesses. This interplay between archetypes allows for a more balanced, adaptable approach to life's challenges.

Perhaps you identify primarily as an **Empowered Trailblazer**, bold and action-oriented, but at times, you are aware that the reflective qualities of the **Reflective Orchestrator** might be needed to temper your decisions with wisdom and patience. Or maybe you embody the **Radiant Alchemist**'s ability to transform pain into purpose, but you could benefit from the **Liberated Voyager**'s adventurous spirit to break free from routine and explore new avenues of growth.

This integration creates a synergy of strength, allowing you to meet each new experience with a broader range of tools. Learning to combine and integrate the qualities and strengths of multiple archetypes can actually serve to provide you with a richer, more dynamic toolkit for holistic healing in response to trauma.

For example, the **Phoenix Riser** thrives on resilience, rising again and again from life's adversities, while the **Resilient Sage** gathers wisdom from each challenge, reflecting on the lessons learned and then using them as stepping stones for growth. Both archetypes are focused on survival and transformation, but they take different approaches. The **Phoenix Riser** leans into action and renewal, while the **Resilient Sage** embraces introspection and learning. By combining these energies, you gain both the power to rise and the insight to grow, turning each setback into an opportunity for lasting personal evolution.

The Synergy of Strengths: Blending Archetypes for Wholeness

What makes blending archetypes so powerful is the ability to shift between different qualities depending on the circumstances. The ability to embody multiple energies not only fosters balance but also creates a deeper sense of adaptability and empowerment. As we know, each archetype carries specific strengths, and when blended, these strengths can amplify one another, creating a more holistic approach to healing and thriving.

Let's dive deeper into how different archetypes can complement each other:

- **The Phoenix Riser**'s resilience in the face of destruction can be balanced by the **Reflective Orchestrator**'s thoughtful planning. While the Phoenix Riser rises quickly from challenges, the Reflective Orchestrator helps ensure that the decisions following recovery are grounded in careful reflection and strategy, providing a roadmap for more sustained success and helping to minimise the risk of burnout.

- **The Authentic Warrior** is focused on truth and vulnerability, but sometimes this raw authenticity needs the **Resilient Sage**'s wisdom to temper it with compassion and empathy. The Warrior is direct and bold in confronting their truth, and the Sage can guide them in approaching their relationships and inner struggles with a gentler, more reflective stance, fostering a deeper sense of connection and understanding.

- **The Liberated Voyager** thrives on exploration and breaking free from patterns, but this energy can benefit from the **Radiant Alchemist**'s ability to transform pain into meaning rather than defaulting to avoidance. The Voyager seeks freedom and new horizons, and the Alchemist ensures that the journey is one of purpose, where personal experiences are harnessed along the way for deeper growth.

This symbiotic dance between archetypes creates not only a stronger foundation for healing but also a more expansive perspective on what it means to move forward and ultimately to thrive after trauma.

Case Studies: The Power of Archetypal Blending in Healing

Let's explore some stories of individuals who have successfully blended archetypal energies in order to foster their own healing and growth. These examples will help you see how combining the qualities of different archetypes can lead to a holistic transformation.

Case Study 1: The Phoenix Riser & The Authentic Warrior

Meet Tash, a survivor of complex trauma who initially identified strongly as a Phoenix Riser. She had rebuilt her life, time and again after each setback, yet still struggled with an ongoing feeling of isolation and loneliness as well as a sense of constantly being in survival mode. After recognising her deep desire for authenticity and connection with both herself and with others, she began to tap into her Authentic Warrior energy.

By integrating this archetype, Tash learned to embrace her vulnerability and started to invite trusted others into her healing process. She not only continued to rise from the adversity but also developed deeper, more meaningful relationships, whilst fighting for her truth and embracing her authentic self, no longer feeling the need to keep that part hidden. This combination allowed Tash to stop viewing her life as one of constant rebuilding and start seeing it as a journey of deeper self-expression and connection.

Case Study 2: The Resilient Sage & The Radiant Alchemist

Greg, a Resilient Sage, was known for his wisdom and insight, often guiding others through difficult times. However, after experiencing significant personal loss, he found himself stuck in reflection, struggling to move forward. Through his journey, Greg began to tap into the transformative power of the Radiant Alchemist.

By engaging in creative practices like writing and his artwork, he was able to turn his pain into purpose, blending the Sage's wisdom with the Alchemist's transformative energy. This combination allowed him not only to heal but also to inspire others through his creative work. For Greg, integrating these archetypes unlocked a deeper level of healing by combining reflection with transformation, allowing him to both honour his past while shaping his future.

Case Study 3: The Empowered Trailblazer & The Reflective Orchestrator

Hayley identified as an Empowered Trailblazer, always leading with courage and breaking new ground in her professional life. However, she often found herself burning out, pushing herself too hard without taking the time to reflect and recharge. By incorporating the qualities of the Reflective Orchestrator, Hayley learned to balance her action-oriented approach with more careful planning and introspection.

This combination enabled her to sustain her leadership, make more thoughtful decisions, and achieve lasting success without sacrificing her well-being. The integration of the Trailblazer's boldness with the Orchestrator's strategic thinking allowed Hayley to continue forging ahead without losing herself in the process.

Practical Applications for Combining Archetypes

The additional bonus is that the process of blending archetypal energies isn't just limited to moments of crisis or to healing from trauma—it can also enhance various aspects of our daily life, from work and relationships to achieving personal goals. Here are some practical ways to apply these combinations:

1. Work and Career

In the workplace, combining the energies of different archetypes can lead to a more effective and fulfilling career. For example, you may be a Liberated Voyager, eager to explore new opportunities and break free from conventional paths. However, drawing on the Reflective Orchestrator can help you to strategise and plan your next move more effectively, ensuring that your adventurous spirit is grounded in thoughtful decision-making.

Alternatively, if you identify as an Empowered Trailblazer, blending in the Radiant Alchemist can help you turn any career setbacks into opportunities for growth and innovation. The Trailblazer's courage paired with the Alchemist's ability to transform challenges into creative solutions can propel you to greater heights.

2. Relationships

Relationships can be another area where blending archetypes means you can create deeper, more meaningful connections. If you resonate with the Authentic Warrior, you may be skilled at standing in your truth and setting boundaries. Integrating the compassionate wisdom of the Resilient Sage can help you approach potential conflict with greater empathy and understanding.

Likewise, if you are a Phoenix Riser, known for your resilience in the face of adversity, blending in the energy of the Liberated Voyager can encourage you to explore new ways of connecting with others, and seeking freedom from past relational patterns. These combined energies can foster both self-respect and compassion, leading to more harmonious and fulfilling relationships overall.

3. Personal Growth

Personal growth is a lifelong journey, and combining the archetypal energies can accelerate that process. If you find yourself primarily identifying with one archetype, ask yourself: What other qualities would support my growth? And how can I look to tap into those qualities of another archetype as effectively as possible?

For instance, if you are a Reflective Orchestrator, you may benefit from tapping into the courage of the Empowered Trailblazer when it comes to taking risks and stepping outside of your comfort zone. Or, if you are a Radiant Alchemist focussed on personal transformation, welcoming in the wisdom of the Resilient Sage can help you make decisions that are grounded in long-term insight.

This blending of archetypes can bring a dynamic balance to your personal growth, ensuring that your transformation is both bold and wise and ultimately more sustainable and successful.

Exercises for Integrating Multiple Archetypes

To help you identify and blend the strengths of your archetypes, I've included a few exercises designed to foster greater self-awareness and further integration.

1. Archetype Reflection Exercise

Take a moment to reflect on the situations in your life that require multiple strengths. Ask yourself: Which archetype do I most naturally lean toward? What other archetypal qualities would complement my approach? Write down how blending these energies might support you in different areas of life.

A tip here might be to look at where the challenges or weaknesses of your primary archetype lie, and you may be able to counteract them by blending an alternative archetype's strength that you don't yet resonate so strongly with.

2. Visualisation Exercise

Imagine a challenge you are currently facing. Visualise yourself embodying the strengths of two or more archetypes. How would your Phoenix Riser resilience work together with your Authentic Warrior authenticity in this situation? How can the Empowered Trailblazer's courage complement the Radiant Alchemist's creativity? Explore how these combined energies can bring new perspectives to the challenge. Lean into whatever comes up for you and trust your inner wisdom.

3. Action Plan

Create an action plan for how you can consciously integrate multiple archetypes into your daily life. For instance, if you are taking on a new project at work, how can the Reflective Orchestrator's strategic planning combine with the Liberated Voyager's boldness to lead you to success? Write down specific actions you can take to embody these blended energies.

Conclusion: Embracing Your Multidimensional, Holistic Path to Healing and Growth

Healing is a deeply personal and multidimensional journey. Just as you are not defined by a single experience or identity, you are not confined to a single archetype. Holistic healing requires you to recognise and honour the many layers of who you are. Each archetype reflects a part of your potential, and by integrating them, you unlock a broader range of strengths, insights, and tools for transformation.

This holistic approach does more than accelerate healing—it empowers you to live with greater authenticity, balance, and purpose. It's about embracing the full spectrum of who you truly are. It allows you to draw from the **Phoenix Riser's resilience**, the **Empowered Trailblazer's courage**, the **Resilient Sage's wisdom**, the **Reflective Orchestrator's strategy**, the **Authentic Warrior's truth**, the **Radiant Alchemist's transformation**, and the **Liberated Voyager's freedom**. Together, these archetypes can guide you toward a life of holistic growth, where each aspect of yourself is nurtured and empowered to thrive.

Remember, healing is not about fitting into a single mould. By blending archetypal energies, you are not just healing one part of yourself—you are inviting balance and alignment across all dimensions of your being. Holistic growth arises when every part of you is honoured and integrated, allowing your mind, body, and spirit to heal in harmony and move you toward a life of holistic growth, healing, and boundless possibility.

As you continue your path to post-traumatic growth, recognise that you are a multidimensional being capable of embodying the diverse strengths of many archetypes. By embracing this integration, you unlock the potential for growth in every area of your life - relationships, career, health, and inner fulfillment.

The journey of growth is ongoing. Each step brings you closer to the most authentic, empowered, and radiant version of yourself. You have the power to rewrite your story, create your own path and draw on the diverse energies within you. Embrace this journey of archetypal integration and watch as your healing expands into every facet of your life, bringing with it newfound strength, peace, and joy.

CHAPTER 14

Beyond Trauma
-
The Future
of Your Growth

"Although the world is full of suffering, it is also full of the overcoming of it."

- Helen Keller

As you reach this final chapter, I want to honour the incredible journey you've taken. You've explored the depths of your trauma and its impact on you, embraced the archetypes that resonate with your experience, and discovered new strengths within yourself. But now, we're looking ahead - moving beyond your trauma. You are no longer defined by the pain you've endured, but by the growth, wisdom, and resilience that have emerged from it. You are moving from being a survivor to being a thriver.

This chapter is an invitation to step fully into your new identity, to continue your journey of self-discovery and growth with courage and confidence. Your trauma may be a part of your story, but it is not the whole of it. You are so much more than the struggles you've faced and endured —you are the architect of your own future.

Moving from Survivor to Thriver

Many of us start our healing journey identifying as survivors. This identity is powerful because it acknowledges our strength, our ability to endure, and the fact that we have made it through something incredibly difficult. Surviving is an essential stage of the healing process because it allows us to reclaim a sense of safety and stability within our lives. We recognise our capacity to persevere, to rebuild, and ultimately to move forward. But surviving isn't the end of the story. Surviving is the beginning of a new chapter - one where you can take charge and move beyond simply existing and start thriving.

Thriving is about embracing life in all its fullness. It's about seeing yourself not just as someone who has overcome trauma, but as someone who is capable of living with purpose, joy, and great passion. Thriving means that your trauma no longer defines you; instead, it has become a catalyst for growth and propelled you forward to transformation. It has given you the tools to fully live authentically, to create meaningful connections, and to chase your dreams without being ruled by fear.

This shift from survivor to thriver is a deeply profound one. It requires you to re-evaluate how you see yourself: not as someone shaped by your past but as someone with limitless potential for the future. The transition from survivor to thriver is not always easy. It requires letting go of old identities that kept you safe but may also have kept you stuck. The identity of survivor - while empowering in its own right - can also tether you to the past, reinforcing a mindset of protection and caution. To thrive, you need to expand beyond that. You need to fully step into a space where you see yourself as capable of happiness, fulfillment, and ultimately of success—not just in *spite* of your trauma, but sometimes *because* of it.

Thriving means living in alignment with your true self, no longer hiding behind fear, shame, or especially self-doubt. It's about daring to dream again and trusting in your ability to create a life that feels authentic and meaningful. It's about allowing yourself to experience joy without the guilt and moving toward your goals with a sense of purpose.

Yet, it's important to acknowledge that the path to thriving isn't linear. There will be moments of doubt, setbacks, and days when you feel like slipping back into survival mode. These moments don't mean you've failed. In fact, they are a normal part of growth. The difference now is that you have the awareness, the tools, and the resilience to navigate these challenges without being consumed by them. You are stronger than you've ever been because you now understand that healing isn't about erasing the past – instead, it's about integrating it in a way that empowers your future.

Embrace the Journey of Self-Discovery and Growth

Even though you've come so far, this journey of self-discovery and growth is an ongoing one. Healing isn't a destination, but rather a continuous process of learning, evolving, and of becoming. The beautiful thing about growth is that it never ends. There is always more to learn, more to explore, and more to experience. Your future is filled with endless possibilities and ample opportunities.

By embracing the journey rather than focusing solely on the outcome, you allow yourself the freedom to grow at your own pace. There's no rush, and indeed there's no finish line. You've developed a deep understanding of yourself through your archetypes. You've recognised your strengths, acknowledged your weaknesses, and understand your potential challenges, and learned to navigate life with greater self-awareness and compassion. Now, I encourage you to continue building on this solid foundation. Keep pushing yourself to grow, to evolve, and to become the best version of yourself.

This journey is not about perfection—it's about progress. It's about honouring your personal evolution and embracing each step, even when it's challenging. Allow yourself to continue growing, not because you need to "fix" anything, but because after all you've been through, you deserve to experience all that life has to offer.

Redefining Your Narrative

As you move from survivor to thriver you will begin to redefine your personal narrative. Trauma no longer dominates the storyline of your life. Instead, it becomes a chapter in a much larger, more complex narrative. One that is filled with moments of joy, hope, love, and possibility.

When trauma first enters our lives, it can feel overwhelming and like it overshadows everything else. It may shape how we see the world, how we see ourselves, and how we engage with others.

But the truth is, trauma is just one part of our stories. It doesn't need to be the defining part.

You are a person of depth, complexity, and incredible potential. Your trauma has shaped you, yes absolutely —but it has not broken you! Instead, it has given you a profound understanding of life, of strength, and of resilience. It has shown you what you're capable of when faced with adversity. Now, it's time to embrace the other parts of your story—the parts filled with joy, hope, love, and possibility.

One of the most empowering aspects of post-traumatic growth is the ability to take control of your own narrative. *You* get to decide how your story unfolds from here. You get to write the next chapters with intention, passion, and a sense of purpose. You are not defined by what has happened to you—you are defined by what you choose to do with it from here.

As you step into your future, consider what kind of story you want to narrate about your life. Do you want to tell a story of resilience, strength, and transformation? Or do you want to hold onto the old narrative of fear, pain, and limitation? The choice is yours. And I know, from everything you've experienced and everything you've learned, that you will create a future filled with possibility, strength, and light.

Trusting Yourself and Your Inner Wisdom

One of the most valuable gifts you've undoubtedly gained on this journey is the ability to trust yourself again. Trauma often robs us of that trust. It makes us doubt our instincts, question our worth, and fear our ability to make decisions. Yet through this healing journey, you've learned to reconnect with your inner wisdom.

You've re-established a relationship with yourself—one built on compassion, understanding, and self-trust. You've come to realise that you are your own best advocate, and you know what's best for you. This newfound trust in yourself is a cornerstone of thriving. It allows you to move forward with confidence, knowing that you are indeed capable of navigating whatever challenges life throws your way.

This doesn't mean you'll never face moments of doubt or uncertainty. We all do. But the difference now is that you have the tools to navigate those moments without being consumed by them. You know how to listen to that inner voice of yours, how to tune into your needs, and how to honour your boundaries. You are no longer at the mercy of your trauma—you are now in control of your own destiny.

The Power of Connection and Community

Another crucial element of thriving is the power of connection and community. Healing from trauma can generally feel like a solitary journey, but true growth happens in connection with others. Whether it's your friends, family, or a supportive community, the people in your life play a vital role in your continued growth.

Surround yourself with individuals who lift you up, who see your potential, and who continuously encourage your growth. These are the people who will remind you of your strength on the days when you forget. They will celebrate your victories and hold space for you during your struggles. Connection with others is a vital part of thriving because it reminds us that we are not alone.

As you continue to move forward, don't be afraid to lean on the people who love and support you. Their presence in your life is a testament to the progress you've made. When you allow yourself to be seen, to be heard, and supported, you open yourself up to even greater growth and transformation.

Building a Life of Meaning and Purpose

As you step into the identity of a thriver, you are not just surviving—you are building a life of meaning, of purpose, and ultimately of fulfillment. Your trauma has given you a unique perspective on life. It has shown you what truly matters, and it has opened your eyes to the things that bring you joy, fulfillment, and peace.

Now is the time for you to build a life that aligns with your values. Whether it's in your relationships, your career, or your personal pursuits, or across all these areas, you can create a life that feels authentic and meaningful to you and a life that truly matters. A life where you are no longer weighed down by the past but propelled forward by the wisdom you've gained.

The Future of Your Growth

As we bring this chapter to a close, I encourage you to look toward your future with excitement and great anticipation. The future of your growth is unlimited. You have all the tools and strategies you need to continue evolving into the person you were always meant to be. You have everything within you to create a life filled with meaning, purpose, and great joy.

Your future is not bound by your past. Instead, it is directed by the wisdom you've gained from it. You are more than a survivor—you are a thriver. You are an empowered, resilient, and radiant being, capable of achieving anything you set your mind to.

So, as you move forward, remember this: You are not your trauma and you are never alone. You are the growth, the wisdom, and the transformation that has come from it. You have your inner strengths, your archetypes, and your community to support you every step of the way.

You are the architect of your own life, and your future is filled with endless possibilities. The journey may not always be easy, but it will always be worth it. Trust in yourself, in your inner wisdom, and in the incredible future that lies ahead.

Embrace your growth, cherish your journey, and step boldly into the future you deserve. You are not just someone who has survived trauma—you are thriving in the face of it. The future is yours to claim, and I have no doubt that it will be extraordinary.

CONCLUSION

Your Path to Thriving

"What lies behind us and what lies before us are tiny matters compared to what lies within us."

— Ralph Waldo Emerson

As we come to the end of this journey together, I want to take a moment to reflect on the incredible path you've travelled. From the depths of trauma to the heights of thriving, you're learning to embrace your unique strengths, face your vulnerabilities, and harness the power of your archetypes to catalyse your healing. You've discovered the essence of Post-Traumatic Growth and how it can transform pain into purpose, fear into freedom, and despair into hope. The transformation you have embarked upon is not just about healing but about thriving—living a life beyond the constraints of your trauma, filled with deeper meaning and profound growth.

Reflecting on the Journey

As you know, the path to thriving is rarely linear. It is a winding road filled with moments of doubt, confusion, hope, and perseverance. You've been through stages of uncertainty, where the future seemed bleak, and your past felt like a burden too heavy to carry. And yet, here you are—standing at the threshold of a new chapter in your life.

This chapter is not marked by your trauma, but by your fortitude, your resilience, your growth, and your transformation. You have journeyed from being a survivor to becoming a thriver, someone who not only overcomes adversity but turns it into a powerful source of inner strength.

Throughout this book, we've explored the seven archetypes—each representing different facets of the human spirit in its quest to overcome adversity. You've seen how the **Phoenix Riser** rises from the ashes, how the **Resilient Sage** turns experience into wisdom, how the **Empowered Trailblazer** forges new paths, and how each archetype embodies a vital part of the healing process. You've recognised that within you lies an **Authentic Warrior**, a **Reflective Orchestrator**, a **Radiant Alchemist**, and a **Liberated Voyager**—all with their own strengths, wisdom, and light and you can draw on each of them as needed.

These archetypes are not just symbols or metaphors; they are aspects of yourself that you have likely connected with, perhaps without even realising. Each one speaks to a different way of processing and overcoming trauma, and they offer a roadmap to the unique ways you can continue to heal and grow.

The Phoenix Riser

The Phoenix Riser symbolises your ability to rise from the ashes of trauma, to rebuild and renew. This archetype teaches you that no matter how devastating your past may be, you have within you the power to recreate yourself. The Phoenix does not emerge unscathed but renewed, stronger, and more resilient.

The journey of rising after trauma is not about forgetting the past, but about allowing it to shape a more powerful version of yourself. This is not only about survival but about becoming someone who thrives—someone who can live fully, joyfully, and purposefully.

The Resilient Sage

The Resilient Sage is the part of you that turns hardship into wisdom. This archetype has taught you that even the darkest experiences carry valuable lessons. It is through pain that we inevitably gain insight, and it is through adversity that we develop compassion, understanding, and wisdom. The Sage within you has shown you how to distil the essence of your experiences into wisdom that will guide you through the rest of your life. As you continue your path, the wisdom of the Sage will serve as your compass, helping you navigate the complexities of life with grace, patience, and inner strength.

The Empowered Trailblazer

The Empowered Trailblazer reminds you that healing is not about returning to who you were before the trauma, but about forging a new path. Trauma changes you, and while that can be painful, it also opens so many new possibilities. The Trailblazer within you is bold, innovative, and fearless in carving out a life that aligns with your newfound understanding of yourself and the world. This archetype empowers you to step into your authentic power, make bold choices, and take risks that will lead to a desired life filled with purpose and passion.

The Reflective Orchestrator

The Reflective Orchestrator is the part of you that seeks balance, harmony, and understanding. This archetype has taught you how to navigate the complexities of your emotions, thoughts, and experiences. It reminds you that healing does not have to be a chaotic process, rather one that requires reflection, integration, and mindfulness. The Orchestrator within you has shown you how to bring together all the different aspects of your life—past, present, and future—into a cohesive whole, allowing you to move forward with clarity and purpose.

The Authentic Warrior

The Authentic Warrior represents the courage to face your inner battles, confront your fears, and embrace your vulnerability. This archetype has guided you in recognising that vulnerability is not a weakness as you may have thought, but indeed a strength. It takes immense bravery to be open, to face your wounds, and to heal. The Warrior within you has given you the strength to fight for yourself, to reclaim your life, and to stand in your truth, no matter how difficult the journey may have been.

The Radiant Alchemist

The Radiant Alchemist is the aspect of you that transforms pain into beauty, fear into love, and despair into hope. This archetype has shown you that within every challenge lies the seed of true transformation. The Alchemist within you is the source of your creative power, reminding you that you can turn even the darkest experiences into something beautiful and meaningful. As you choose to continue your path to thriving, the Alchemist will help you transmute your past into the fuel that ignites and powers your future, lighting up your life with joy, creativity, and fulfillment.

The Liberated Voyager

Finally, the Liberated Voyager is the part of you that seeks freedom—freedom from the chains of the past, freedom to explore new horizons, and freedom to live authentically and fully. The Voyager within you is driven by a deep desire for liberation, for breaking free from those old patterns and limitations that have held you back. This archetype encourages you to embrace the unknown, to step outside your comfort zone, and to trust in your ability to navigate whatever challenges lie ahead. The Voyager will guide you toward a future that is expansive, adventurous, and filled with possibility.

A Lifelong Journey of Growth

But this journey doesn't end here. The path to thriving is a lifelong one. Healing, growth, and transformation are not finite destinations; they are ongoing processes.

Every day presents an opportunity to deepen your relationship with yourself, to harness the power of your archetypes, and to take another step toward the life you choose to live. Some days will be easier than others, and there will be times when old wounds resurface, or new challenges arise. But each time, know that you will have the tools, the strategies, the inner wisdom, and the strength to face whatever comes your way.

Growth is not about perfection—it's about progress. It's about showing up for yourself, day after day, with self-compassion, patience, and determination. There will be setbacks, but they do not define you. What defines you is your ability to rise after each fall, to learn from each experience, and to keep moving forward, no matter how slow or difficult the journey may seem.

A Message of Hope and Encouragement

As someone who has faced trauma and emerged out the other side, I want you to know that your future is bright, and it is absolutely filled with possibility. No matter how dark your past has been, you have the power to create a future that is abundant with joy, purpose, and fulfillment. You are not defined by what has happened to you; you are defined by what you choose to do with it. And I know, without a doubt, that you are capable of the most extraordinary things.

This book is just the beginning of your journey. You've already proven to yourself that you have the resilience, the strength, and the courage to heal and grow. Now, as you move forward, I encourage you to continue to honour your growth, to embrace the lessons of your archetypes, and to trust in your capacity to thrive.

Deepen Your Work with the Archetypes

If these pages have resonated and you feel called to continue exploring your archetypes on a deeper level, I invite you to join me in the next phase of your journey. There are many ways you can deepen your work with the archetypes and further accelerate your growth, whether it's through personalised coaching, or our online group programs.

I've created these additional resources to provide ongoing support, so you never feel alone on your path to thriving. My mission is to empower you, every step of the way, to break free from the chains of trauma and to step into the fullness of your potential. Ideally my greatest desire is to end the *suffering* attached to trauma in the world. Healing is not a solitary endeavour—it's a journey we take together. And I am honoured to walk this path with you.

Your Path to Thriving

As you close this book and step boldly into the future, remember this: you are more powerful than you could ever imagine and my wish for you is to have this realisation. You are capable of transforming not just your life, but the lives of others. Your story, your journey, and your growth have the power to inspire change far beyond what you can see. Every time you choose to rise, to heal, and to thrive, you are lighting the way for others to do the same.

So, continue to nurture your growth, to honour your archetypes, and to embrace the fullness of who you are becoming. The path to thriving is yours to walk—and with every step, you are creating a life that is rich with meaning, with purpose, and with possibility.

The future is bright, and it is yours to claim. I'm cheering you on every step of the way.

With endless hope and the deepest belief in you, I can't wait to see you shining your light brightly in the world.

References

Dell'Osso, L., Carmassi, C., Rossi, R., & Bianchi, I. (2022). Post-Traumatic Growth and Resilience in Individuals with PTSD: A Systematic Review. *Journal of Affective Disorders*, 299, 120-135.

Dell'Osso L, Lorenzi P, Nardi B, Carmassi C, Carpita B. (2022) Post Traumatic Growth (PTG) in the Frame of Traumatic Experiences. *Clin Neuropsychiatry, 19(6),* 390-393. doi: 10.36131/cnfioritieditore20220606. PMID: 36627947; PMCID: PMC9807114.

Furness, J.B. (2012). The Enteric Nervous System: Normal Functions and Enteric Pathology. *Gut, 57(6),* 860-869. doi:10.1136/gut.2008.170688.

Green, N. (2017). *Key to Freedom: The 7 Step Model to Triumph Over Trauma.* Melbourne: Busybird Publishing.

Green, N. (2024). From Both Sides of the Couch: Revolutionising Trauma Healing. In *Empowered Women Empower Women.* Melbourne: Changemaker Press.

Oka, M., & Soosalu, G. (2012). *mBIT (multiple Brain Integration Techniques) Coaching Workbook.* mBIT International Pty Ltd.

Oka, M., & Soosalu, G. (2012). *MBraining: Using Your Multiple Brains to Do Cool Stuff.* Timebinding Publications

Van der Kolk, B. (2014). *The Body Keeps the Score: Brain, Mind, and Body in the Healing of Trauma.* New York: Viking.

About The Author

Dr Nat Green is a Trauma Breakthrough Coach, Bestselling Author and Podcast host with a background in Clinical and Health Psychology. She is passionate about transforming lives and revolutionising the trauma landscape.

With over 30 years' working in trauma, and having lived experienced with trauma, Dr Nat is an industry trailblazer. She is the author of 'Key to Freedom - The 7-Step Model to Triumph Over Trauma' and Creator and Founder of the Accelerated Breakthrough Strategies (ABS) Method™, which accelerates trauma healing and facilitates transformation into post traumatic growth.

She was a nominee in the 2024 International Women in Podcasting Awards in the USA, received an Award at the Therapists Rising Industry Awards in 2023, and has been accepted into the AUSCEP program for 2025 for her revolutionary work in trauma using the ABS Method® and Archetypes of Transformation© work.

When she isn't writing, podcasting or changing lives Dr Nat enjoys coffee by the beach and travelling. She lives on the NSW Mid North Coast with her husband, and two kids.

Get in Contact with Dr Nat :

Email: drnat@drnataliegreen.com.au
Facebook: https://www.facebook.com/DrNatalieGreen
Instagram: https://www.instagram.com/drnatgreen/
Website: www.drnataliegreen.com.au
Podcast: Growing Tall Poppies
Get The Quiz: https://drnataliegreen.com.au/trauma-archetypes-quiz

www.ingramcontent.com/pod-product-compliance
Lightning Source LLC
Chambersburg PA
CBHW061734070526
44585CB00024B/2664